"I immediately went to my nurse manager after I failed the NCLEX® and she referred me to ATI. I was able to discover the areas I was weak in, and focused on those areas in the review modules and online assessments.

I was much more prepared the second time around!"

Terim Richards
Nursing student

Danielle Platt
Nurse Manager • Children's Mercy Hospital • Kansas City, MO

"The year our hospital did not use the ATI program, we experienced a 15% decrease in the NCLEX® pass rates. We reinstated the ATI program the following year and had a 90% success rate."

"As a manager, I have witnessed graduate nurses fail the NCLEX® and the devastating effects it has on their morale. Once the nurses started using ATI, it was amazing to see the confidence they had in themselves and their ability to go forward and take the NCLEX® exam."

Mary Moss
Associate Dean of Nursing - Service and Health Division • Mid-State Technical College • Wisconsin Rapids, WI

"I like that ATI lets students know what to expect from the NCLEX®, helps them plan their study time and tells them what to do in the days and weeks before the exam. It is different from most of the NCLEX® review books on the market."

Editor

Jeanne Wissmann, PhD, RN, CNE
Director of Nursing Curriculum and Educational Services
Assessment Technologies Institute®, LLC

Associate Editors

Jamie Easum, BSN, RN
Educational Services Coordinator

Kristen M Lawler, MBA
Director of Development

Derek Prater, MS Journalism
Product Developer

Advisory Reviewers

Wendy Buenzli, MSN, RN
Penny Fauber, PhD, RN
Jackie Jones, EdD, RN

Important Notice to the Reader of this Publication

Assessment Technologies Institute®, LLC is the publisher of this publication. The publisher reserves the right to modify, change, or update the content of this publication at any time. The content of this publication, such as text, graphics, images, information obtained from the publisher's licensors, and other material contained in this publication are for informational purposes only. The content is not providing medical advice and is not intended to be a substitute for professional medical advice, diagnosis, or treatment. Always seek the advice of your primary care provider or other qualified health provider with any questions you may have regarding a medical condition. Never disregard professional medical advice or delay in seeking it because of something you have read in this publication. If you think you may have a medical emergency, call your primary care provider or 911 immediately.

The publisher does not recommend or endorse any specific tests, primary care providers, products, procedures, processes, opinions, or other information that may be mentioned in this publication. Reliance on any information provided by the publisher, the publisher's employees, or others contributing to the content at the invitation of the publisher, is solely at your own risk. Health care professionals need to use their own clinical judgment in interpreting the content of this publication, and details such as medications, dosages or laboratory tests and results should always be confirmed with other resources.

This publication may contain health or medical-related materials that are sexually explicit. If you find these materials offensive, you may not want to use this publication.

The publishers, editors, advisors, and reviewers make no representations or warranties of any kind or nature, including, but not limited to, the accuracy, reliability, completeness, currentness, timeliness, or the warranties of fitness for a particular purpose or merchantability, nor are any such representations implied with respect to the content herein (with such content to include text and graphics), and the publishers, editors, advisors, and reviewers take no responsibility with respect to such content. The publishers, editors, advisors, and reviewers shall not be liable for any actual, incidental, special, consequential, punitive, or exemplary damages (or any other type of damages) resulting, in whole or in part, from the reader's use of, or reliance upon, such content.

Preface

Overview

The overall goal of this Assessment Technologies Institute®, LLC (ATI) Content Mastery Series module is to provide nursing students with an additional resource for the review of "Nutrition for Nursing Practice" content relevant to NCLEX® preparation and entry level nursing practice. Content within this review module is provided in a key point plus rationale format in order to focus recall and application of relevant content. Unit and chapter selections are reflective of the nutrition-relevant content categories and content explanations of the NCLEX® test plans, the ATI "Nutrition for Nursing Practice" assessment test plans, and standard nursing curricular content. Each chapter begins with an overview of some of the topic-relevant nursing activities outlined by the NCLEX® test plans in an effort to guide the learner's review and application of chapter content.

Contributors

ATI would like to extend appreciation to the nurse educators and nurse specialists who contributed content for this review module. The names of contributors are noted in the chapter bylines. We would also like to thank those talented individuals who reviewed, edited, and developed this module. Additionally, we want to recognize and express appreciation to all of the contributors, reviewers, production developers, and editors of previous editions of this Content Mastery Series module.

Suggestions for Effective Utilization

- As a review of NCLEX®-relevant content in developing and assessing readiness for NCLEX®.

- As a review resource based on the results of an ATI "Nutrition for Nursing Practice" assessment. "Topics to Review" for these assessments will guide learners to chapter(s) within this review module. To foster long-term recall and development of an ability to apply knowledge to a variety of situations, learners are encouraged to take a comprehensive approach to topic review. Using this review module along with other resources (class notes, course textbooks, nursing reference texts, instructors, ATI DVD series), consider exploration of the topic, addressing questions such as:

  ◊ What are the components of a quality nutritional assessment? Why?

  ◊ What are rich dietary sources of a specific nutrition component? Identify similarities among sources.

  ◊ What are factors that enhance nutrient metabolism? Decrease nutrient metabolism? Identify why and note patterns among factors.

  ◊ What are the guidelines for healthy eating and what is a nurse's role in health promotion regarding nutrition?

  ◊ What are parameters for the safe preparation and storage of foods?

  ◊ What are some common food-medication interactions? What are interventions to prevent or reduce the impact of these interactions?

  ◊ What are the specific nutritional needs of individuals across their lifespan (during pregnancy, lactation, infancy, childhood, adolescence, adulthood, and older adulthood)? Identify three to four age-appropriate nutritional priorities. For each priority, identify specific food sources to encourage or discourage.

  ◊ Identify foods that can be included in each of the hospital diets (clear liquid, full liquid, pureed, mechanical soft, and soft diets).

  ◊ Identify sources of enteral nutrition. Outline a nurse's role in safe, effective provision of enteral nutrition. Identify possible complications and presenting signs and symptoms. For each complication, identify nursing interventions to prevent and/or respond appropriately.

◊ Identify sources of parenteral nutrition. Outline a nurse's role in safe, effective provision of parenteral nutrition. Identify possible complications and presenting signs and symptoms. For each complication, identify nursing interventions to prevent and/or respond appropriately.

◊ Identify dietary changes appropriate for specific diagnoses. Categorize diagnoses with similar dietary changes. Categorize dietary changes, for example increased intake of fiber. For each dietary change, identify specific foods to encourage or discourage. Be able to apply this knowledge to the provision of special diets, the provision of health teaching regarding dietary changes, and to the monitoring of a client's compliance and/or need for further dietary instruction.

◊ What client findings (laboratory results, weight, intake and output) indicate a need for dietary alteration? What client findings should be monitored and why? What client findings indicate effective dietary alteration?

• Complete application exercises at the end of each chapter after a review of the topic. Answer questions fully and note rationales for answers. Complete exercises initially without looking for the answers within the chapter or consulting the answer key. Use these exercises as an opportunity to assess your readiness to apply knowledge. When reviewing the answer key, in addition to identifying the correct answer, examine why you missed or answered correctly each item – was it related to ability to recall, recognition of a common testing principle, attention to key words?

Feedback

All feedback is welcome – suggestions for improvement, reports of mistakes (small or large), and testimonials of effectiveness. Please address feedback to: comments@atitesting.com

Unit 1   Principles of Nutrition

Chapter 1:   Nutritional Assessment

Contributor: Marsha L. Ray, MSN, RN

↻ NCLEX® Connections:

Learning Objective: Review and apply knowledge within **"Nutritional Assessment"** in readiness for performance of the following nutrition nursing activities as outlined by the NCLEX® test plans:

Δ   Consider the client's nutritional preferences.

Δ   Evaluate and/or monitor the impact of disease/illness on the client's nutritional status through completion of a diet history.

Δ   Monitor the client's hydration status.

Δ   Monitor the client's weight.

Δ   Collect a diet history from the client.

✎ Key Points

Δ   Nurses play a key role in assessing the **nutritional needs** of the client.

•   Nurses monitor and intervene with clients requiring **acute** and **chronic** nutritional care.

•   The family's **nutritional habits** must be considered and incorporated into an individual client's care.

•   Nurses should take an active role in surveying and teaching community groups regarding nutrition.

Δ   A **collaborative multidisciplinary approach** provides the best outcomes for the client.

•   Physical assessment data is collected by providers and nurses.

•   Comprehensive **nutritional assessments** are completed by registered dieticians.

•   Nurses monitor and evaluate **interventions** provided to clients.

Δ   A client's physical appearance can be deceiving.

- Even a client with a healthy look and weight can be malnourished.

- Comparison to cultural, social, and physical norms must be part of a client's assessment.

Δ   Even with adequate client education, personal preferences can be an overriding factor to successful nutritional balance.

Nursing Assessments/Data Collection and Interventions

Diet History

Δ   A diet history is an assessment of **usual foods, fluids,** and **supplements**. Components include:

- **Time, type, and amount** of each **food** eaten for breakfast, lunch, dinner, and snacks.

- Time, type, and amount of **fluids** consumed throughout the day, including water, health drinks, coffee/tea, carbonated beverages, and beverages with caffeine.

- Type, amount, and frequency of **"special foods"** (celebration foods, movie foods).

- Typical **preparation** of foods and fluids (coffee with sugar, fried foods).

- Number of meals eaten away from home.

- Type of **normal diet** (lacto-ovo-vegetarian, 2 g sodium/low-fat diet).

- **Foods avoided** either due to allergy or preference.

- Frequency and dose/amount of **medications** or nutritional supplements taken daily.

- **Satisfaction** with diet over a specified time frame (last 3 months, last year).

Assessment Tools to Determine Nutritional Status

Δ   **Physical assessment** is performed by the provider or nurse to identify indicators of inadequate nutrition. Remember, these signs and symptoms can be caused by other processes/diseases/conditions. **Symptoms** include:

- Hair that is dry, dull, or brittle, and/or skin that has dry patches.

- Poor **wound healing** or sores.

- Lack of subcutaneous fat and/or **muscle wasting**.

- **Abnormal cardiovascular measurements** (heart rate and rhythm, blood pressure).

- **General weakness** and/or impaired coordination.

Δ   **Anthropometric Tools**

•   **Weight**

◊   Weigh at the same time of day wearing similar clothing to ensure accurate weight.

◊   Daily fluctuations are generally indicative of water weight changes.

◊   **Percentage weight change calculation** (weight change over a specified time):
usual weight – present weight x 100
        usual weight

°   1 to 2% in 1 week indicates significant weight loss.

°   7.5% in 3 months indicates significant weight loss.

◊   **"Ideal" body weight** based on height (plus or minus 10% depending on frame size).

°   For males, this is 48 kg (106 lb) for the first 152 cm (5 ft) of height and 2.7 kg (6 lb) for each additional 2.5 cm (1 inch).

°   For females, this is 45 kg (100 lb) for the first 152 cm (5 ft) of height and 2.3 kg (5 lb) for each additional 2.5 cm (1 inch).

•   **Height**

◊   Young children and infants should be measured lying on a firm, flat surface.

•   **Body Mass Index** (BMI) – Normal/healthy is 18.5 to 24.9.

◊   BMI = weight (kg) ÷ height (m²)

•   **Body Fat Composition Methods**

◊   Skin-fold measurement

◊   Waist-to-hip ratio

◊   Densitometry (underwater weighing)

Δ **Clinical Values**

•   Fluid Intake and Output (I&O)   normal daily range

Intake 2,200–2,700 mL   Output 2,200–2,700 mL   In 24 hr

- **Protein levels** are measured commonly by serum albumin levels as a general measure. Many non-nutritional factors, such as injury or renal disease, hamper this measure for protein malnutrition.

- **Prealbumin** (thyroxin-binding protein) is a more sensitive measure used to assess critically ill clients who are at high risk for malnutrition. This test reflects more acute changes versus gradual changes.

Clinical Laboratory Tests	Normal	Moderate Depletion
Albumin	3.5 to 5.5 g/dL	2.1 to 2.7 g/dL
Prealbumin	23 to 43 mg/dL	5 to 9 mg/dL

Risk Factors for Inadequate Nutrition

Δ Biophysical Factors

- Medical disease/condition/treatment, such as hypertension or surgery

- Genetic predisposition, such as lactose intolerance or osteoporosis

- Age

Δ Psychological Factors

- Mental illness, such as clinical depression

- Excessive stress

- Negative self-concept

- Use of comfort foods

Δ Socioeconomic Factors

- Poverty

- Alcohol and drug abuse

- Fad or "special" diets

- Food preferences: cultural, ethnic, religious

Δ Impact of Risk Factors on Nutritional Status

- The following are examples of how risk factors can affect nutritional status.

  ◊ The client is **edematous** and requires treatment with a diuretic and a low-sodium diet. Diuretics can cause sodium and potassium imbalances. A low-sodium diet may be unappetizing and cause inadequate consumption.

  ◊ **Osteoporosis** has many modifiable risk factors, such as calcium and vitamin D intake, inactive lifestyle, cigarette smoking, or alcohol intake. Altering these risk factors can affect nutritional status in a positive manner.

◊ **Poor self-concept** could cause the client to avoid needed foods/nutrients or to eat too much.

◊ The client practices a **traditional** cultural **foodway** (see Chapter 5) that is high in meat proteins and fats. These foods can put the client's nutritional status at risk.

Primary Reference:

Dudek, S. G. (2006). *Nutrition essentials for nursing practice* (5th ed.). Philadelphia: Lippincott Williams & Wilkins.

Additional Resources:

Potter, P. A., & Perry, A. G. (2005). *Fundamentals of nursing* (6th ed.). St. Louis, MO: Mosby.

Chapter 1: Nutritional Assessment

Application Exercises

Scenario: A 19-year-old female client who recently broke her wrist is at the eating disorder clinic for a twice-a-week appointment. The nurse smells a strong odor of cigarette smoke on her clothes. Her slender mother anxiously states: "The ER doctor said that the cast weighs 10 oz. She is now using her broken wrist as an excuse to spend more time in her bed or on the couch." Her records indicate that she is 173 cm (5 ft 8 in) tall, and the scales indicate a weight of 50 kg (110 lb).

1. Determine this client's BMI.

2. Calculate the client's percentage weight change using her ideal body weight as her base weight.

3. Outline what the nurse should teach this client regarding her risk for osteoporosis.

4. Which of the following laboratory values suggests moderate protein deficiency for an acutely ill client?

    A. Serum albumin, 3.5 g/dL

    B. Serum prealbumin, 5 mg/dL

    C. Serum albumin, 4.5 g/dL

    D. Serum prealbumin, 10 mg/dL

5. Which of the following client findings is most suggestive of malnutrition for an older adult?

    A. Wrinkles, dry skin, and small but protuberant abdomen

    B. Halting gait, sagging neck skin, and thin legs

    C. Blood pressure 130/80 mm Hg, pedal edema, and cheerful

    D. Lack of subcutaneous fat, brittle hair, and weak handgrips

6. Develop one specific question to ask a client for each of the following diet history components.

Diet History Component	Client Question
Time, type, and amount of each food eaten for breakfast, lunch, dinner, and snacks	"Tell me what time you usually eat breakfast and what you usually eat. I'll give you an example: I typically eat at 7 a.m. and have either two pieces of buttered toast and 8 oz of orange juice or 1 cup of hot oatmeal with ½ banana and 10 oz of non-fat milk with 1 Tbsp of cocoa mixed in it."
Time, type, and amount of fluids consumed throughout the day (water, health drinks, coffee/tea, carbonated beverages, and beverages with caffeine)	
Type, amount, and frequency of "special foods" (celebration foods, movie foods)	
Typical preparation of foods and fluids (coffee with sugar, fried foods)	
Number of meals eaten away from home	
Type of normal diet (lacto-ovo-vegetarian, 2 g sodium/low-fat diet)	
Foods avoided either due to allergy or preference	
Frequency and dose/amount of medications or nutritional supplements taken daily	
Satisfaction with diet over a specified time frame (last 3 months, last year)	

7. Describe a recording tool that the client could use to gather the information needed to analyze his nutritional intake.

Chapter 1: Nutritional Assessment

Application Exercises Answer Key

Scenario: A 19-year-old female client who recently broke her wrist is at the eating disorder clinic for a twice-a-week appointment. The nurse smells a strong odor of cigarette smoke on her clothes. Her slender mother anxiously states: "The ER doctor said that the cast weighs 10 oz. She is now using her broken wrist as an excuse to spend more time in her bed or on the couch." Her records indicate that she is 173 cm (5 ft 8 in) tall, and the scales indicate a weight of 50 kg (110 lb).

1. Determine this client's BMI.

$$170 \text{ cm} = 1.7 \text{ meters}$$

$$\text{BMI} = \frac{\text{weight (kg)}}{\text{height (m}^2\text{)}}$$

$$= \frac{50}{1.7^2} = \frac{50}{2.89} = 17.3$$

2. Calculate the client's percentage weight change using her ideal body weight as her base weight.

Ideal body weight: 5 ft 8 in = 45 kg + (2.3 kg x 8) = 63.4 kg

([base weight – new weight] ÷ base weight) x 100

([63.4 – 50] ÷ 63.4) x 100

(13.4 ÷ 63.4) x 100 = 21.1%

3. Outline what the nurse should teach this client regarding her risk for osteoporosis.

Δ   Osteoporosis runs in families, and the client's mother is slender; therefore, the client might have an increased risk for osteoporosis.

Δ   Cigarette smoking can increase the incidence of osteoporosis (or make it worse); therefore, smoking cessation should be encouraged with community/medical referral.

Δ   There is an increased risk due to inactivity; therefore, weight-bearing exercise should be planned.

Δ   Weight loss can cause a decreased intake of dietary calcium and vitamin D; therefore, the client's diet should be evaluated for a possible increase in dietary calcium and vitamin D.

4. Which of the following laboratory values suggests moderate protein deficiency for an acutely ill client?

> A. Serum albumin, 3.5 g/dL
> **B. Serum prealbumin, 5 mg/dL**
> C. Serum albumin, 4.5 g/dL
> D. Serum prealbumin, 10 mg/dL

Answer "B" is indicative of a moderate depletion of protein. The serum prealbumin test, also known as thyroxin-binding protein, is most sensitive to acute changes in protein nutrition. Serum albumin levels reflect slow changes in serum protein levels, not acute serum protein changes.

5. Which of the following client findings is most suggestive of malnutrition for an older adult?

> A. Wrinkles, dry skin, and small but protuberant abdomen
> B. Halting gait, sagging neck skin, and thin legs
> C. Blood pressure 130/80 mm Hg, pedal edema, and cheerful
> **D. Lack of subcutaneous fat, brittle hair, and weak hand grips**

Answer "D" describes changes reflective of malnutrition. All other descriptors can be attributed to the normal aging process.

6. Develop one specific question to ask a client for each of the following diet history components.

Diet History Component	Client Question
Time, type, and amount of each food eaten for breakfast, lunch, dinner, and snacks	"Tell me what time you usually eat breakfast and what you usually eat. I'll give you an example: I typically eat at 7 a.m. and have either two pieces of buttered toast and 8 oz of orange juice or 1 cup of hot oatmeal with ½ banana and 10 oz of non-fat milk with 1 Tbsp of cocoa mixed in it."
Time, type, and amount of fluids consumed throughout the day (water, health drinks, coffee/tea, carbonated beverages, and beverages with caffeine)	"Describe what type of fluid you drink throughout the day and what size of glass or cup you use." "Tell me what you drink for breakfast, lunch, and dinner." "How many cups of coffee do you drink a day?" "Do you drink carbonated beverages, such as Pepsi or 7-Up?"

Diet History Component	Client Question
Type, amount, and frequency of "special foods" (celebration foods, movie foods)	"When you go to the movie theater, what do you buy to eat and drink? What size do you buy?" "When you are celebrating something special with your family, what special foods do you eat?"
Typical preparation of foods and fluids (coffee with sugar, fried foods)	"Do you like your meat and chicken dishes baked, broiled, pan fried, deep-fat fried, or barbecued?" "Do you put a lot of salt on your foods when you eat or when you cook it?" "How much sugar do you use each day?"
Number of meals eaten away from home	"How many times do you go out to eat each week?" "Do you pack your lunch from home or buy it at or near your workplace?"
Type of normal diet (lacto-ovo-vegetarian, 2 g sodium/low-fat diet)	"Do you eat a special diet, like a low-fat diet?" "Do you eat both vegetables and meat?" "Are you a vegan?" "Do you eat Kosher?"
Foods avoided either due to allergy or preference	"Are there any foods that you are allergic to?" "Does any food give you a rash, make you itch, or cause your tongue or throat to swell?" "Is there any type of food that you won't eat? What is it?"
Frequency and dose/amount of medications or nutritional supplements taken daily	"Please list the time and amount of all medications that you use daily." "Do you use any supplements, health food tablets, herbs, or diet supplements? Which ones and how often?"
Satisfaction with diet over a specified time frame (last 3 months, last year)	"Are you happy with the way you have been eating for the last 3 months?" "Have you changed the foods you eat over the last year? Why?"

7. Describe a recording tool that the client could use to gather the information needed to analyze his nutritional intake.

Diet log: Record all foods, times, and portions (amounts) of items consumed in the last 3 days, or week, or month.

Diet recall: List all foods/fluids consumed in the past 24 hr.

Unit 1   Principles of Nutrition

Chapter 2:   Sources of Nutrition: Carbohydrates & Fiber, Protein, Lipids, Vitamins, Minerals & Electrolytes, and Water

Contributor: Sue Kilgore, RN

⟳ **NCLEX® Connections:**

Learning Objective: Review and apply knowledge within **"Sources of Nutrition: Carbohydrates & Fiber, Protein, Lipids, Vitamins, Minerals & Electrolytes, and Water"** in readiness for performance of the following nutrition nursing activities as outlined by the NCLEX® test plans:

Δ   Complete calorie counts for clients.

Δ   Assess and/or monitor the hydration status of the client.

Δ   Provide/maintain special diets and/or nutritional supplements based on the client's diagnosis/nutritional needs.

📖 **Key Points**

Δ   Components of **nutritive sources** are carbohydrates & fiber, protein, lipids (fats), vitamins, minerals & electrolytes, and water.

Δ   Nutrients absorbed in the diet determine, to a large degree, the health of the body. Deficiencies or excesses can contribute to a poor state of health.

Δ   **Essential nutrients** are those that the body cannot manufacture. The absence of essential nutrients causes deficiency diseases.

Δ   Carbohydrates, fats, and proteins are **energy-yielding nutrients**.

Δ   The **Dietary Reference Intakes** (DRIs), developed by the Institute of Medicine's Food and Nutrition Board, is the most commonly used source on nutrient allowances for healthy people. Formerly known as the **Recommended Dietary Allowances** (RDAs), the DRIs comprise four reference values: RDAs, Estimated Average Requirements (EARs), **Adequate Intakes** (AIs), and Tolerable Upper Intake Levels (ULs).

Carbohydrates & Fiber

All carbohydrates are **organic compounds composed of carbon, hydrogen, and oxygen** (CHO). The main function of carbohydrates is to provide energy for the body.

Δ   The **average minimum** amount of carbohydrates needed to fuel the brain is **130 g/day**. Median carbohydrate intake is 200 to 330 g/day among men and 180 to 230 g/day among women, and the acceptable macronutrient distribution range for carbohydrates is 45 to 65% of calories.

Δ   Carbohydrates **provide energy** for cellular work. They help regulate protein and fat metabolism. They are essential for normal cardiac and central nervous system (CNS) functioning.

Δ   Carbohydrates are classified according to the number of saccharide units making up their structure:

- **Monosaccharides** are simple carbohydrates (glucose, fructose).

- **Disaccharides** are simple carbohydrates (sucrose, lactose).

- **Polysaccharides** are complex carbohydrates (starch, fiber, glycogen).

Δ   As **complex carbohydrates** are ingested and broken down, they are easily absorbed in the intestine and into the bloodstream where they are stored in the liver and muscles for energy needs.

Δ   The body absorbs 80 to 95% of carbohydrates. Absorption occurs mainly in the small intestine using pancreatic and intestinal enzymes.

Δ   **Glycogen** is the stored carbohydrate energy source found in the liver and muscles. It is a vital source of backup energy.

Δ   Carbohydrate foods are generally widely available, easily grown, and have long storage times.

Δ   Carbohydrates provide 4 cal/g of energy.

Δ   **Fiber** is categorized as a carbohydrate, but does not yield energy for the body.

- Dietary fiber is the substance in plant foods that is indigestible. Types are: **pectin, gum, cellulose, and mucilage**.

- Fiber is important for **proper bowel elimination**. It adds bulk to the feces and will stimulate peristalsis to ease elimination.

- Studies show fiber also helps to lower cholesterol and lessen the incidence of intestinal cancers.

Types of Carbohydrates

Type	Monosaccharides	Disaccharides	Polysaccharides
Example/(Sources)	Glucose (corn syrup), fructose (fruits), galactose (milk sugar broken down)	Sucrose (table sugar, molasses), lactose (milk sugar), maltose (sweeteners)	Starches (grains, legumes, root vegetables), fiber (indigestible plant parts)
Function	Basic energy for cells	Energy, aids calcium and phosphorus absorption (lactose)	Energy storage (starches), digestive aid (fiber)

Proteins

Proteins are provided by plant and animal sources. They are formed by **linking amino acids** in various combinations for specific use by the body.

Δ   There are **three types** of proteins – complete, incomplete, and complementary – and they are obtained from the diet in various ways.

    •   **Complete** proteins, generally from animal sources, contain all of the essential amino acids (there are 9 essential amino acids).

    •   **Incomplete** proteins, generally from plants (grains, nuts, legumes, vegetables, fruits), do not contain all of the essential amino acids. Vegetarians require a variety of plant materials in specific combinations in order to ensure essential amino acid intake.

    •   **Complementary** proteins are those food sources that, when eaten together, provide all the essential amino acids.

Δ   Proteins have many **metabolic functions** such as: tissue building and maintenance, balance of nitrogen and water, backup energy, support of metabolic processes (nitrogen balance, transportation of nutrients and other vital substances), and support of the immune system.

Δ   Three main factors influence the body's requirement for protein: (1) tissue growth needs, (2) quality of the dietary protein, and (3) added needs due to illness.

Δ   The **recommended dietary requirement** of protein for adults is **10% of intake**, or 46 g/day for women and 56 g/day for men.

Δ   Undernutrition can lead to protein malnourishment, which can lead to kwashiorkor or marasmus. These are serious disorders caused by lack of protein ingestion or metabolism resulting in a cachectic (wasting) state.

Δ   Protein provides 4 cal/g of energy.

Lipids

The **chemical group of fats** is called lipids, and they are available from many sources, such as dark meat, poultry skin, dairy foods, and added oils (margarine, butter, shortening, oils, and lard).

Δ   **Fat is an essential body nutrient**. It serves as a concentrated form of energy for the body (second to carbohydrates) and supplies important tissue needs, such as hormone production, structural material for cell walls, protective padding for vital organs, insulation to maintain body temperature, covering for nerve fibers, and aid in the absorption of fat-soluble vitamins.

Δ   Fats are divided into the following categories: triglycerides, phospholipids, sterols, saturated fats, unsaturated fats, polyunsaturated fats, and essential fatty acids.

   •   **Triglycerides** (the chemical name for fats) are the primary form of fat in food. They combine with glycerol to supply energy to the body, allow fat-soluble vitamin transport, and form adipose tissue that protects the body.

   •   **Phospholipids** are derived from triglycerides. They are important to cell membrane structure.

   •   **Cholesterol** belongs to the chemical substance group called sterols. It is necessary for cell membrane stability and the production of certain hormones and bile salts for digestion. If cholesterol is consumed in excess, it can build up in the tissues causing congestion and increasing the risk for cardiovascular disease.

   •   **Saturated fats** are of animal origin. Fats from plant sources usually are unsaturated fats and help reduce health risks (notable exceptions are coconut and palm oil).

   •   **Essential fatty acids**, made from broken down fats, must be supplied by the diet. Essential fatty acids, including omega-3 and omega-6, are used to support blood clotting, blood pressure, inflammatory responses, and many other metabolic processes.

   •   **Linoleic acid** is an important essential fatty acid and is found primarily in polyunsaturated vegetable oils.

Δ   Generally, **no more than 20 to 35% of total calories should come from fat** (10% or less from saturated fat sources).

   •   A high-fat diet is linked to cardiovascular disease, hypertension, and diabetes mellitus.

   •   The exception to this rule is for children under 2 years of age, who need higher amounts of fat to form brain tissue.

Δ   Conversely, a diet with less than 10% fat cannot supply adequate amounts of essential fatty acids and results in a cachectic (wasting) state.

Δ   The majority of **lipid metabolism** occurs after fat reaches the small intestine, where the gallbladder secretes concentrated bile that acts as an emulsifier to break fat into smaller particles. At nearly the same time, the pancreas secretes pancreatic lipase, which breaks down fat. The small intestine also secretes an enzyme for further breakdown. The muscles, liver, and adipose tissue cause the release of fatty acids, and the liver also produces lipoproteins to carry lipids.

- **Very Low Density** Lipoproteins (**VLDL**) carry triglycerides to the tissues.

- **Low Density** Lipoproteins (**LDL**) carry cholesterol to the tissues.

- **High Density** Lipoproteins (**HDL**) remove excess cholesterol from the tissues. HDL is considered the "good" cholesterol.

Δ   Lipids provide 9 cal/g of energy and are the densest form of stored energy.

Vitamins

Vitamins are organic substances required for many enzymatic reactions. The main function of vitamins is as catalysts for metabolic functions and chemical reactions.

Δ   There are **13 essential vitamins**, each having specialized functions.

Δ   The two classes of vitamins are:

- Water-soluble – Vitamins C and B-complex

- Fat-soluble – Vitamins A, D, E, and K

Δ   Vitamins yield no usable energy for the body.

Water-Soluble Vitamins

Δ   **Vitamin C** (ascorbic acid) aids in tissue building and many metabolic reactions, such as wound and fracture healing, collagen formation, adrenaline production, iron absorption, conversion of folic acid, and cellular adhesion.

- Vitamin C is found in citrus fruits (oranges, lemons), tomatoes, peppers, green leafy vegetables, and strawberries.

- Stress and illness increase the need for this antioxidant.

- Severe deficiency causes scurvy, a hemorrhagic disease with diffuse tissue bleeding, painful limbs/joints, weak bones, and swollen gums/loose teeth.

Δ   **B-complex vitamins** have many functions in cell metabolism. Each one has varied "duties." Many "partner" with other B vitamins for metabolic reactions. Most affect energy, metabolism, and neurological function. Sources for B vitamins almost always include green leafy vegetables and unprocessed or enriched grains.

- **Thiamin (B$_1$)** is necessary for proper digestion and peristalsis and providing energy for smooth muscles, glands, the CNS, and blood vessels.

  ◊   Deficiency results in beriberi, gastrointestinal symptoms, and cardiovascular problems.

  ◊   Food sources are widespread in almost all plant and animal tissues, especially meats, grains, and legumes.

- **Riboflavin** (B_2) is required for growth, vitality, and tissue healing.

  ◊ Deficiency results in cheilosis (manifestations include scales and cracks on lips and mouth), smooth/swollen red tongue, and dermatitis, particularly in skin folds.

  ◊ Dietary sources include milk, meats, and green leafy vegetables.

- **Niacin** (B_3) aids in energy and protein metabolism.

  ◊ Deficiency can cause pellagra (manifestations include sun-sensitive skin lesions and gastrointestinal and neurologic symptoms).

  ◊ Sources include beef liver, nuts, and legumes.

- **Pantothenic acid** (B_5) is involved in a number of biological reactions, including the production of energy, catabolism, and synthesis of fatty acids, phospholipids, cholesterol, steroid hormones, and the neurotransmitter acetylcholine.

  ◊ Deficiency results in anemia and CNS changes; however, deficiency is unlikely due to the diverse availability in foods.

  ◊ Rich sources include organ meats (liver, kidney), egg yolk, avocados, cashew nuts and peanuts, brown rice, soy, lentils, broccoli, and milk.

- **Pyridoxine** (B_6) is needed for cellular function and synthesis of hemoglobin, neurotransmitters, and niacin.

  ◊ Deficiency causes anemia and CNS disturbances.

  ◊ High intake of supplements may cause sensory neuropathy.

  ◊ Widespread food sources include organ meats and grains.

- **Biotin** serves as a coenzyme used in fatty acid synthesis, amino acid metabolism, and the formation of glucose.

  ◊ Deficiency is rare but can result in neurological symptoms (depression, fatigue) and rashes on the skin, especially the face ("biotin deficient face").

  ◊ Widespread food sources include eggs, milk, and dark green vegetables.

- **Folate** (**folic acid** is the synthetic form) is required for hemoglobin and amino acid synthesis, cellular reproduction, and prevention of neural tube defects in utero.

  ◊ Deficiency causes megaloblastic anemia, CNS disturbances, and fetal neural tube defects (such as spina bifida and anencephaly). It is important that all women of child-bearing age get an adequate amount of folate due to neural tube formation occurring early in gestation, often before a woman knows she is pregnant.

  ◊ Folate occurs naturally in a variety of foods, including liver, dark-green leafy vegetables, citrus fruits, whole-grain products, and legumes.

- **Cobalamin** (B_{12}) is necessary for the production of red blood cells.

  ◊ Deficiency causes pernicious anemia and is seen mostly in strict vegetarians (since B_{12} is found solely in foods of animal origin) and those with the absence of intrinsic factor needed for absorption of B_{12}.

  ◊ Sources include beef liver, mollusks, and fortified grains.

Water-Soluble Vitamins at a Glance

	Ascorbic Acid Vitamin C	Thiamin B$_1$	Riboflavin B$_2$	Niacin B$_3$	Pantothenic Acid B$_5$	Pyridoxine B$_6$	Folate	Cobalamin B$_{12}$
Major Actions	Antioxidant, tissue building, iron absorption	Muscle energy, GI support, CV support	Growth, energy, tissue healing	Energy and protein metabolism/ cellular metabolism	Fatty acid metabolism, cell synthesis, heme production	Cellular function, heme & neurotransmitter synthesis	Synthesis of amino acids & hemoglobin, lower neural tube defect in fetus	Hemo-globin synthesis
Major Sources	Citrus fruits and juices, vegs	Meats, grains, legumes	Milk, meats, green leafy vegs	Liver, nuts, legumes	Organ meats, egg yolk, avocados, broccoli	Organ meats, grains	Liver, green leafy vegs, grains, legumes	Organ meats, clams, oysters, grains
Infants (AI)	40-50 mg	0.2-0.3 mg	0.3-0.4 mg	2-4 mg	1.7-1.8 mg	0.1-0.3 mg	65-80 µg	0.4-0.5 µg
RDA Children (age 1-8)	15-25 mg	0.5-0.6 mg	0.5-0.6 mg	6-8 mg	2-3 mg	0.5-0.6 mg	150-200 µg	0.9-1.2 µg
RDA Adolescent (age 9-18)	45-75 mg	0.9-1.2 mg	0.9-1.3 mg	12-16 mg	4-5 mg	1-1.3 mg	300-400 µg	1.8-2.4 µg
RDA Adult Male	90 mg	1.2 mg	1.3 mg	16 mg	5 mg	1.3-1.7 mg	400 µg	2.4 µg
RDA Adult Female	75 mg	1.1 mg	1.1 mg	14 mg	5 mg	1.3-1.5 mg	400 µg	2.4 µg
RDA Female Pregnant/ Lactating	80-85 mg/ 115-120 mg	1.4 mg/ 1.4 mg	1.4 mg/ 1.6 mg	18 mg/ 17 mg	6 mg/ 7 mg	1.9 mg/ 2.0 mg	600 µg/ 500 µg	2.6 µg/ 2.8 µg
Deficiency	Scurvy, decreased iron absorption	Beriberi, altered digestion, CNS & CV problems	Skin eruptions, cracked lips, red swollen tongue	Pellagra, skin lesions, GI & CNS symptoms	Anemia, CNS changes	Anemia, CNS hyper-irritability, neuritis	Megalo-blastic anemia, CNS disturbance	Pernicious anemia

Source: Food and Nutrition Information Center. *Dietary Reference Intakes (DRI) and Recommended Dietary Allowances (RDA).* Retrieved May 4, 2006, from http://www.nal.usda.gov/fnic/etext/000105.html

Fat-Soluble Vitamins

Δ   All fat-soluble vitamins have the possibility for toxicity due to their ability to be stored in the body for long periods.

Δ   Absorption of fat-soluble vitamins depends on the body's ability to absorb dietary fat.

- Fat digestion can be interrupted by any number of conditions, particularly those that affect the secretion of fat-converting enzymes and conditions of the small intestine. Therefore, clients with cystic fibrosis, celiac disease, Crohn's disease, or intestinal bypasses are at risk for deficiencies.

Δ   Clients with liver disease should be careful not to overdose with fat-soluble vitamins, as levels can build up.

Δ   **Vitamin A** (retinol, beta-carotene) contributes to vision health, tissue strength and growth, and embryonic development.

- Care should be taken when administering to pregnant females, as some forms have teratogenic effects on the fetus.

- Deficiency can result in vision changes, xerophthalmia (dryness and thickening of the conjunctiva), and changes in epithelial cells (especially in the mouth and vaginal mucosa).

- Food sources include fish liver oils, egg yolks, butter, cream, and dark yellow/orange fruits and vegetables (carrots, yams, apricots, squash, cantaloupe).

Δ   **Vitamin D** (calciferol) assists in the utilization of calcium and phosphorus and aids in skin repair.

- Deficiency results in bone demineralization, and extreme deficiency results in rickets. Clients on glucocorticoid therapy may require additional amounts. Excess consumption may cause hypercalcemia.

- Food sources include fortified milk, cod liver oil, and eggs.

- Sunlight enables the body to synthesize vitamin D.

Δ   **Vitamin E** (tocopherol), an antioxidant, helps preserve muscle and red blood cells and maintains the myelin sheath that insulates nerve cells.

- Deficiency results in hemolytic anemia and affects the nerve fibers that influence walking and vision.

- Food sources include vegetable oils, eggs, avocados, and certain nuts.

Δ **Vitamin K** (menaquinone, phylloquinone) assists in blood clotting and in bone maintenance.

- Deficiency results in increased bleeding time.

- It is found in some oils, liver, and in green leafy vegetables such as spinach, broccoli, and cabbage. The typical American diet provides adequate amounts.

- Used as an antidote for excess anticoagulants, such as warfarin (Coumadin).

Fat-Soluble Vitamins at a Glance

	Vitamin A	Vitamin D	Vitamin E	Vitamin K
Major Actions	Normal vision, tissue strength, growth and tissue healing	Maintain serum calcium and phosphorus, which aid in bone development	Protects cells from oxidation	Normal blood clotting (prothrombin production), aids in bone metabolism
Major Sources	Orange/yellow colored foods, liver, fish oils, dairy	Fish, fish liver oil, fortified dairy products, sunlight	Vegetable oils, grains, nuts, eggs	Green leafy vegs, plant oils, liver
Infants (AI)	400-500 µg	5 µg	4-5 mg	2-2.5 µg
RDA Children (age 1-8)	300-400 µg	5 µg	6-7 mg	30-55 µg
RDA Adolescent (age 9-18)	600-900 µg	5 µg	11-15 mg	60-75 µg
RDA Adult Male	900 µg	5-15 µg	15 mg	120 µg
RDA Adult Female	700 µg	5-15 µg	15 mg	90 µg
RDA Female Pregnant/ Lactating	750-770 µg/ 1,200-1,300 µg	5 µg/ 5 µg	15 mg/ 19 mg	75-90 µg/ 75-90 µg
Deficiency	Reduced night vision, dry/thick eyes, mucosa changes	Low serum calcium, fragile bones, rickets	Hemolytic anemia, CNS changes	Increased bleeding times

Source: Food and Nutrition Information Center. *Dietary Reference Intakes (DRI) and Recommended Dietary Allowances (RDA)*. Retrieved May 4, 2006, from http://www.nal.usda.gov/fnic/etext/000105.html

Minerals & Electrolytes

Minerals are available in an abundance of food sources; they are used at every cellular level for metabolic exchanges.

Δ   Minerals are divided into major and trace.

•   **Major minerals** occur in larger amounts in the body.

•   **Trace elements**, also called micronutrients, are required by the body in amounts less than 100 mg/day.

Δ   The **seven major minerals** are: calcium, phosphorus, sodium, potassium, magnesium, chloride, and sulfur.

Δ   The **ten trace elements** that are essential are: iron, iodine, zinc, copper, manganese, chromium, cobalt, selenium, molybdenum, and fluoride.

Δ   **Electrolytes** are electrically charged minerals that cause physiological reactions that maintain homeostasis. The most commonly monitored electrolytes are: sodium, potassium, chloride, calcium, and magnesium. They affect many disease processes.

Major Minerals at a Glance

	Sodium (AI)	Potassium (AI)	Chloride (AI)	Calcium (AI)	Magnesium (RDA*)	Phosphorus (RDA*)	Sulfur
Major Actions	Maintains fluid volume, allows muscle contractions, cardiovascular support	Maintains fluid volume inside/outside cells, muscle action, blood pressure, cardiovascular support	Bonds to other minerals (esp. sodium) to facilitate cellular actions and reactions, fluid balance	Bones/teeth, cardiovascular support, blood clotting, nerve transmission	Bone nourishment, catalyst for many enzyme reactions, nerve/muscle function, CV support	Energy transfer of RNA/DNA, acid-base balance	Role in acid-base balance
Major Sources	Table salt, added salts, processed foods, butter	Oranges, dried fruits, tomatoes, avocados, dried peas, meats, broccoli, bananas	Table salt	Dairy, broccoli, kale, grains, egg yolks	Green leafy vegs, nuts, grains, meat, milk, "hard water"	Dairy, peas, soft drinks, meat, eggs, some grains	Readily available in water and other organics (dried fruits, meats, wines)

	Sodium (AI)	Potassium (AI)	Chloride (AI)	Calcium (AI)	Magnesium (RDA*)	Phosphorus (RDA*)	Sulfur
Infants (AI)	0.12-0.37 g	0.4-0.7 g	0.18-0.57 g	210-270 mg	30-75 mg	100-275 mg	None established
Children (age 1-8)	1-1.2 g	3.0-3.8 g	1.5-1.9 g	500-800 mg	80-130 mg	460-500 mg	None established
Adolescent (age 9-18)	1.5 g	4.5-4.7 g	2.3 g	1,300 mg	240-410 mg	1,250 mg	None established
Adult Male	1.2-1.5 g	4.7 g	1.8-2.3 g	1,000-1,200 mg	400-420 mg	700 mg	None established
Adult Female	1.2-1.5 g	4.7 g	1.8-2.3 g	1,000-1,200 mg	310-320 mg	700 mg	None established
Female Pregnant/ Lactating	1.5 g/ 1.5 g	4.7 g/ 5.1 g	2.3 g/ 2.3 g	1,000-1,300 mg/1,000-1,300 mg	350-400 mg/ 310-360 mg	700-1,250 mg/ 700-1,250 mg	None established
Deficiency Risks	Excess perspiration, persistent vomiting/ diarrhea or other fluid loss, shock	Diuresis, some medications	Excess perspiration, persistent vomiting/ diarrhea or other fluid loss, shock	Lactose intolerance, GI surgery, parathyroid dysfunction, pancreatitis, renal failure	Excessive vomiting and diarrhea, diabetes malabsorption, renal failure	Unlikely due to vast availability, infant receiving TPN, alcoholism, chronic use of aluminum antacids	Seen only in severe protein mal-nourishment
Deficiency Symptoms	Muscle cramping, cardiac changes	Dysrhythmias, muscle cramps, confusion	Rare	Osteoporosis, tetany, Chvostek's & Trousseau's signs, ECG changes	Weakness, dysrhythmias, tetany, seizure, reduced blood clotting, eclampsia	Calcium level changes, muscle weakness	None known
Complications of Excess	Fluid retention, hypertension, CVA	Dysrhythmias (caused by: supplements, potassium-sparing diuretics, ACE inhibitors, inadequate kidney function, diabetes)	In concert with sodium, results in high blood pressure	Constipation, kidney stones	Diarrhea, kidney stones, decreased muscle control, CV changes	Skeletal porosity, decreased calcium levels, must stay in balance with calcium	N/A
Nursing Implications	Monitor ECG, edema, blood pressure.	Monitor ECG, muscle tone. PO tabs irritate GI. Give with meals.	Monitor sodium levels.	Monitor ECG, muscle tone. Give PO tabs with vitamin D.	Incompatible with some antibiotics. Give PO, 2 hr apart.	Evaluate use of antacids (note type) and use of alcohol.	Interventions focus on replenishment of protein stores.

*Values for infants are AIs.
Source: Food and Nutrition Information Center. *Dietary Reference Intakes (DRI) and Recommended Dietary Allowances (RDA)*. Retrieved May 4, 2006, from http://www.nal.usda.gov/fnic/etext/000105.html

Δ   **Select Trace Minerals**

- **Sulfur**, a component of vitamin structure and a by-product of protein metabolism, is a major mineral and is readily available in water and other organic sources.

  ◊   It is not often monitored in a client's blood level. Sulfur has a role in acid-base balance.

  ◊   Deficiency is only seen in severe protein malnourishment, as sulfur is found in all protein-containing foods.

  ◊   Food sources include dried fruits (dates, raisins, apples), meats, and red and white wines. The RDA is not established due to the common availability of sulfur.

- **Iodine** is used for synthesis of thyroxine, the thyroid hormone that helps regulate metabolism. Iodine is taken up by the thyroid. When iodine is lacking, the thyroid gland enlarges, creating a **goiter**.

  ◊   Grown food sources vary widely and are dependent on the iodine content of the soil in which they were grown.

  ◊   Seafoods provide a good amount of iodine. Table salt in the United States is fortified with iodine, so deficiencies are not as prevalent.

  ◊   The RDA is 100 to 150 μg for adults.

- **Iron** is responsible for hemoglobin formation/function, cellular oxidation of glucose, antibody production, and collagen synthesis.

  ◊   The body "scavenges" unused iron from dying red blood cells and stores it for later use.

  ◊   Iron supplements can cause constipation, nausea, vomiting, diarrhea, and teeth discoloration (liquid form). They should be taken with food to avert gastrointestinal symptoms, and nurses should encourage fresh fruits and vegetables and a high-fiber diet to combat this.

  ◊   Supplements that are unneeded can become toxic.

  ◊   Intramuscular injections are caustic to the tissues and must be administered by Z-track method.

  ◊   Food sources include organ meats, egg yolks, whole grains, and green leafy vegetables.

  ◊   Vitamin C increases the absorption of iron.

  ◊   The greatest need for iron is in the newborn who is not breastfed and for females during the menstruating years.

- **Fluoride** forms a bond with calcium and thus accumulates in calcified body tissue such as bones and teeth. Water with added fluoride protects against dental cavities. Nurses should teach clients who prefer to drink bottled water that they may need fluoride treatments from their dentist.

Water

Water is **the most basic of nutrients**. Whereas the body can maintain itself for several days (even weeks) on its food stores of energy, it cannot survive without water/hydration for more than a few days. Water makes up the largest portion of our total body weight and is crucial for all fluid and cellular function.

Δ **Fluid balance** is essential for optimum health and bodily function.

Δ The balance of fluid is a dynamic process regulated by the release of hormones that regulate body fluid.

Δ To maintain a balance between intake and output, intake should approximate output. The minimum daily total fluid output in healthy adults is 1,500 mL. Therefore, the **minimum daily amount of water needed is 1,500 mL**.

Δ Under normal conditions, recommended adult fluid intake is **3 to 4 L/day for men** and **2 to 3 L/day for women**. It is recommended that half be from water.

Δ Additional hydration may be required for athletes, persons with fever/illness (vomiting, diarrhea), and those in hot climate conditions.

Δ Young children and older adults dehydrate more rapidly.

Δ Clients who must withhold fluids in preparation for a procedure or who cannot hold down fluids may be hydrated with intravenous fluids.

Δ Water leaves the body via the kidneys, skin, lungs, and feces. The greatest elimination is through the kidneys. Other loss factors that must be taken into consideration include: bleeding, vomiting, and rapid respirations. Persistent vomiting can quickly dehydrate a person.

Δ A balanced **input/output ratio** is almost 1:1. One should consider the health status and individual needs of the client.

Δ **Assessment for proper hydration** should include skin turgor, mental status, orthostatic blood pressures, urine output and concentration, and moistness of mucous membranes.

Δ Thirst is a late sign of the need for hydration, especially in older adults.

Δ Some people may have an aversion to drinking plain water. They should be encouraged to explore other options such as: fresh fruits, fruit juices, flavored gelatin, frozen treats, and soups.

Δ Caffeinated drinks have a diuretic effect and should not be substituted for other drinks.

Primary Reference:

> Dudek, S. G. (2006). *Nutrition essentials for nursing practice* (5th ed.). Philadelphia: Lippincott Williams & Wilkins.

Additional Resources:

> Grodner, M., Long, S., & DeYoung, S. (2004). *Foundations and clinical applications of nutrition: A nursing approach* (3rd ed.). St. Louis, MO: Mosby.

> Mitchell, M. K. (2003). *Nutrition across the life span* (2nd ed.). Philadelphia: W.B. Saunders Company.

> Peckenpaugh, N. J., & Poleman, C. M. (2003). *Nutrition essentials and diet therapy* (9th ed.). Philadelphia: W. B. Saunders Company.

> Wardlaw, G. M., & Kessel, M. W. (2002). *Perspectives in nutrition* (5th ed.). St. Louis, MO: Mcgraw-Hill.

> Williams, S. R., & Schlenker, E. D. (2005). *Essentials of nutrition and diet therapy* (8th ed.). St. Louis, MO: Mosby.

> For more information on DRIs, visit the Food and Nutrition Information Center presented by the United States Department of Agriculture's National Agricultural Library at: *www.nal.usda.gov/fnic/*.

Chapter 2: Sources of Nutrition

Application Exercises

1. Which of the following food choices is the most appropriate for a client taking iron supplements?

    A. Liver, baked potatoes, and apple juice

    B. Chicken, spinach salad, and an orange

    C. Pizza and a glass of milk

    D. Pork chops, green beans, and a soda

2. Clients unable to be out in the sunlight can increase their intake of vitamin D by consuming which of the following foods?

    A. Tacos and rice

    B. Hamburgers and fried potatoes

    C. Ham and Brussels sprouts

    D. Eggs and milk

3. An older adult client is prescribed warfarin (Coumadin), an anticoagulant, due to a previous heart attack. Because of the clotting effects associated with vitamin K, the nurse should advise this client to limit intake of which of the following?

    A. Orange juice

    B. Broccoli

    C. Ice cream

    D. Chicken

4. A marathon bicycle rider had an accident a week ago. The client has multiple scrapes to the upper and lower extremities; some are partial-thickness skin wounds. To promote healing, the nurse should suggest which of the following?

    A. Soy protein shakes

    B. Liver and onions

    C. Multi-vitamin tablets

    D. Granola bars

5. Match the following electrolytes and minerals to their food sources.

Electrolyte	Food
_____Potassium	A. Soda pop
_____Sodium	B. Tomatoes
_____Calcium	C. Canned soup
_____Phosphorus	D. Yogurt

6. Match the following health problems with their associated nutrient deficiencies.

Health Problem	Nutrient Deficiency
_____Dysrhythmias	A. Vitamin C
_____Scurvy	B. Potassium
_____Pernicious anemia	C. Folate
_____Megaloblastic anemia	D. Vitamin B_{12}

Chapter 2: Sources of Nutrition

Application Exercises Answer Key

1. Which of the following food choices is the most appropriate for a client taking iron supplements?

        A. Liver, baked potatoes, and apple juice

        B. Chicken, spinach salad, and an orange

        C. Pizza and a glass of milk

        D. Pork chops, green beans, and a soda

Iron supplements should be taken with food to avoid gastrointestinal upset. Vitamin C aids in the absorption of iron, and the orange is a good source of vitamin C. Iron can also cause constipation, so fresh fruits and vegetables are indicated. The spinach salad is a green leafy vegetable and is a good source of natural iron.

2. Clients unable to be out in the sunlight can increase their intake of vitamin D by consuming which of the following foods?

        A. Tacos and rice

        B. Hamburgers and fried potatoes

        C. Ham and Brussels sprouts

        D. Eggs and milk

Sunlight helps to synthesize vitamin D, so these clients need egg yolks and fortified milk, which are both good sources of vitamin D.

3. An older adult client is prescribed warfarin (Coumadin), an anticoagulant, due to a previous heart attack. Because of the clotting effects associated with vitamin K, the nurse should advise this client to limit intake of which of the following?

        A. Orange juice

        B. Broccoli

        C. Ice cream

        D. Chicken

Broccoli is a green leafy vegetable and is a good source of vitamin K. This client should avoid excess vitamin K because it has a negating effect on the warfarin effects.

4. A marathon bicycle rider had an accident a week ago. The client has multiple scrapes to the upper and lower extremities; some are partial-thickness skin wounds. To promote healing, the nurse should suggest which of the following?

      A. Soy protein shakes

      B. Liver and onions

      C. Multi-vitamin tablets

      D. Granola bars

During wound healing, tissue-building needs are increased. Protein helps to rebuild injured tissue. Multi-vitamin tablets are also a good choice since the client's metabolic needs have increased, but they do not have any protein in them for tissue re-generation.

5. Match the following electrolytes and minerals to their food sources.

Electrolyte	Food
B Potassium	A. Soda pop
C Sodium	B. Tomatoes
D Calcium	C. Canned soup
A Phosphorus	D. Yogurt

6. Match the following health problems with their associated nutrient deficiencies.

Health Problem	Nutrient Deficiency
B Dysrhythmias	A. Vitamin C
A Scurvy	B. Potassium
D Pernicious anemia	C. Folate
C Megaloblastic anemia	D. Vitamin B$_{12}$

Unit 1   Principles of Nutrition

Chapter 3:   Factors Affecting Metabolism
                Contributor: Kathleen Jones, MEd, RN

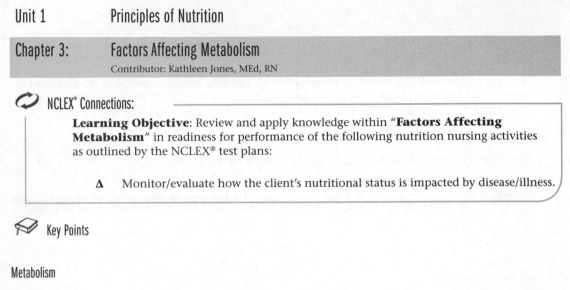

NCLEX® Connections:

Learning Objective: Review and apply knowledge within "**Factors Affecting Metabolism**" in readiness for performance of the following nutrition nursing activities as outlined by the NCLEX® test plans:

Δ   Monitor/evaluate how the client's nutritional status is impacted by disease/illness.

Key Points

Metabolism

Δ   **Metabolism** is the sum of all chemical processes that occur on a cellular level to maintain homeostasis of the body. Food nutrients must enter a cell in order for metabolism to occur.

Δ   Metabolism comprises two processes: **catabolism**, the breaking down of substances with the resultant release of energy, and **anabolism**, the use of energy to build or repair substances.

Δ   Energy nutrients are metabolized to provide carbon dioxide, water, heat, and adenosine triphosphate (ATP).

Δ   Excess energy nutrients are stored: Glucose is converted to **glycogen** and stored in the liver and muscle tissue; surplus glucose is converted to fat; glycerol and fatty acids are reassembled into triglycerides and stored in adipose tissue; and amino acids make body proteins. The liver removes excess amino acids and utilizes the residue to either form glucose or store it as fat.

Δ   Body cells first use available **ATP** for growth and repair and then utilize glycogen and stored fat.

Metabolic Rate

Δ **Metabolic rate** refers to the rate at which food energy is burned. **Basal metabolic rate (BMR)**, also called **resting energy expenditure (REE)**, refers to the amount of energy used when the body is at **rest**.

Δ **BMR** is primarily affected by lean body mass and hormones. Body surface area, age, and gender are minor factors in that they relate to body mass index (BMI).

Factors Affecting BMR	Increase	Decrease
Lean, muscular body build	✔	
Short, overweight body build		✔
Starvation/undernutrition		✔
Exposure to extreme cold	✔	
Prolonged stress	✔	
Rapid growth periods (infancy, puberty)	✔	
Pregnancy	✔	
Lactation	✔	
Over 60 years of age		✔
Physical conditioning	✔	

Δ In general, men have a higher metabolic rate than women because of their higher amount of body muscle and decreased amount of fat.

Δ **Thyroid** function tests may be used as an indirect measure of BMR.

Δ **Acute stress** causes an increase in metabolism, blood glucose levels, and protein catabolism.

- The major nutritional concern during acute stress is protein deficiency, since the stress hormones break down protein at a very rapid rate.

- **Protein deficiency** increases the risk of complications from severe trauma or critical illness, such as skin breakdown, delayed wound healing, infections, organ failure, ulcers, and impaired drug tolerance.

- **Protein requirements** may be increased to 2.0 g/kg of body weight, dependent on the client's age and prior nutritional status.

- **Inadequate protein intake** prevents the body from adapting to physiologic stress.

Δ   **Alcohol** is more quickly metabolized and absorbed than nutrients. Alcohol metabolism changes liver cells and reduces the liver's ability to metabolize fat. Alcoholics suffer from protein-energy malnutrition, generally consuming only about 75% of their energy requirements, which results in low to normal albumin levels.

Δ   Any **catabolic illness** (surgery, extensive burns) increases the body's requirement for calories to meet demands of an increased BMR.

The following diseases affect metabolic rate:		
Disease	Increases Metabolism	Decreases Metabolism
Fever	✔	
Involuntary muscle tremors, as in shivering or Parkinson's	✔	
Hypothyroidism		✔
Hyperthyroidism	✔	
Cancer	✔	
Cardiac failure	✔	
Some anemias	✔	
Hypertension	✔	
Chronic obstructive pulmonary disease	✔	
Burns	✔	
Surgery/wound healing	✔	
HIV/AIDS	✔	

Several medications affect the body's rate of metabolism:		
Medication	Increases BMR	Decreases BMR
Growth hormone	✔	
Prednisone (Deltasone)	✔	
Cortisol	✔	
Epinephrine	✔	
Thyroxine	✔	
Synthroid	✔	
Glucagon	✔	
Ephedrine	✔	
Nortriptyline		✔

Nitrogen Balance

Δ   Nitrogen balance refers to **the difference between the daily intake of nitrogen and nitrogen excretion**. It is also an indicator of tissue integrity. A healthy adult experiencing a stable weight is in nitrogen equilibrium, also known as neutral nitrogen balance.

Δ   **Positive nitrogen balance** indicates that the intake of nitrogen exceeds excretion. In other words, the body is building more tissue than it is breaking down. This normally occurs during periods of growth: infancy, childhood, adolescence, pregnancy, and lactation.

Δ   **Negative nitrogen balance** indicates that the excretion of nitrogen exceeds nitrogen intake. The individual is receiving insufficient protein, and the body is breaking down more tissue than it is building, as in illness, trauma, immobility, and undernutrition.

Δ   **Clinical signs of negative nitrogen balance** are not immediately evident. Decreased muscle tissue, impaired organ function, and increased susceptibility to infection are late signs.

Nursing Assessments/Data Collection

Δ   Weight and history of recent weight patterns

Δ   Medical history for diseases that affect metabolism and nitrogen balance

Δ   Extent of traumatic injuries, as appropriate

Δ   Fluid and electrolyte status

Δ   Abnormal laboratory values: albumin, transferrin, glucose, creatinine

Δ   Clinical signs of malnutrition: pitting edema, hair loss, wasted appearance

Δ   Medication side effects that can affect nutrition

Δ   Usual 24-hr diet intake

Δ   Use of nutritional supplements, vitamins, minerals

Δ   Use of alcohol, caffeine, and nicotine

Nursing Interventions

Δ   Provide adequate calories and high quality protein. Strategies to increase protein and caloric content include:

- Add skim milk powder to milk (double strength milk).
- Substitute whole milk for water in recipes.
- Add cheese, peanut butter, chopped hard-cooked eggs, or yogurt to foods.
- Dip meats in eggs or milk and coat with bread crumbs before cooking.

Δ   Monitor food intake.

Δ   Monitor fluid intake and output.

Primary Reference:

Dudek, S. G. (2006). *Nutrition essentials for nursing practice* (5th ed.). Philadelphia: Lippincott Williams & Wilkins.

Chapter 3: Factors Affecting Metabolism

Application Exercises

1. Indicate the likely nitrogen balance status of the following individuals. Use (+) for positive balance, (-) for negative balance, and (=) to indicate nitrogen equilibrium.

   _____ Olympic skater

   _____ Healthy young adult

   _____ Infant

   _____ Adult with metastatic cancer

   _____ Body builder

   _____ Burn victim

   _____ Breastfeeding mom

2. **True or False:** Individuals experiencing a fever require fewer calories. Explain.

3. **True or False:** A malnourished surgical client is at risk for delayed wound healing. Explain.

4. **True or False:** Serum albumin levels are a reliable indicator of nitrogen balance. Explain.

5. **True or False:** Basal metabolic activities include maintaining normal body temperature, pulse, and respiration. Explain.

6. **True or False:** Older adults require an increase in calories. Explain.

7. List foods appropriate for a client who is immobilized because of bilateral femur and tibia fractures.

Chapter 3: Factors Affecting Metabolism

Application Exercises Answer Key

1. Indicate the likely nitrogen balance status of the following individuals. Use (+) for positive balance, (-) for negative balance, and (=) to indicate nitrogen equilibrium.

   __+__ Olympic skater

   __=__ Healthy young adult

   __+__ Infant

   __-__ Adult with metastatic cancer

   __+__ Body builder

   __-__ Burn victim

   __+__ Breastfeeding mom

2. **True or False:** Individuals experiencing a fever require fewer calories. Explain.

   False: Fever increases metabolic demand. More calories are indicated.

3. **True or False:** A malnourished surgical client is at risk for delayed wound healing. Explain.

   True: Protein deficiency (malnutrition, stress of surgery) increases the risk for delayed wound healing.

4. **True or False:** Serum albumin levels are a reliable indicator of nitrogen balance. Explain.

   True: Nitrogen balance is determined by protein sufficiency. Serum albumin levels are a measurement of serum protein levels.

5. **True or False:** Basal metabolic activities include maintaining normal body temperature, pulse, and respiration. Explain.

   True: Basal metabolic activities maintain body homeostasis.

6. **True or False:** Older adults require an increase in calories. Explain.

    False: Metabolic rate decreases after age 60. Decreased caloric intake is indicated.

7. List foods appropriate for a client who is immobilized because of bilateral femur and tibia fractures.

    Nutrient-dense, high-quality protein foods are appropriate, such as milk shakes, yogurt, egg, turkey, chicken, lean beef, orange juice, strawberries, whole grains, and dark green leafy vegetables.

Unit 1   Principles of Nutrition

Chapter 4:   Health Promotion: Guidelines for Healthy Eating
Contributor: Kathleen Jones, MEd, RN

⟳ NCLEX® Connections:

Learning Objective: Review and apply knowledge within "**Health Promotion: Guidelines for Healthy Eating**" in readiness for performance of the following nutrition nursing activities as outlined by the NCLEX® test plans:

Δ   Assist/encourage the client to achieve and maintain an optimal level of health.

Δ   Instruct and evaluate the client/family/significant other or reinforce client understanding of health risks and on ways to promote health and prevent disease.

Δ   Encourage client participation in appropriate behavior modification programs related to health and wellness.

📖 Key Points

Δ   Nutrition is vital to optimal health. Health promotion and disease prevention are major themes of ***Healthy People 2010***. Healthy food choices, weight control, and reduction of risk factors for disease are specific objectives included in the report.

Dietary Guidelines for Americans

Δ   The U.S. Department of Agriculture (USDA) and the U.S. Department of Health and Human Services (HHS) publish **the Dietary Guidelines for Americans** jointly every 5 years. It provides research-based advice concerning food intake and physical activity for healthy Americans over 2 years of age.

Δ   The Dietary Guidelines for Americans advocates **healthy food selections**: a variety of fiber-rich fruits and vegetables, whole grains, low-fat or fat-free milk and milk products, lean meats, poultry, fish, legumes, eggs, and nuts. Recommendations include:

•   **Balance energy intake with energy expenditure** by selecting a wide variety of foods and limiting saturated and transaturated fat, sugars, sodium, and alcohol.

- **Establish exercise routines** to promote cardiovascular health, muscle strength and endurance, and psychological well-being.

- Increase consumption of **fiber-rich fruits and vegetables** to a minimum of **five servings a day** to decrease risk factors for certain cancers. The vitamin and mineral content of these foods may decrease the risk of DNA damage and cancer.

- Choose **monounsaturated and polyunsaturated fats** from fish and lean meats, nuts, and vegetable oils. Fat intake may average 30% of total caloric intake, with less than 10% from saturated fats.

- **Limit sugar and starchy foods** to decrease the incidence of dental caries.

- Consume **less than 2,300 mg of salt a day** (about 1 tsp) by limiting most canned and processed foods. Prepare foods without adding salt.

- If drinking alcohol, do so in moderation: up to one drink a day for women, two a day for men, as appropriate. Certain medical conditions, medication therapies, and physical activities preclude the use of alcohol.

- **Practice food safety** guidelines when preparing, cooking, and storing food. Avoid consumption of raw eggs and unpasteurized milk and juices.

The Food Guide Pyramid

Δ   The new Food Guide Pyramid, **MyPyramid**, was created in 2005 by the USDA as a visual tool that promotes healthy food choices balanced with physical activity (*www.MyPyramid.gov*).

Δ   Colored food bands represent the proportion and variety of food groups that healthy individuals over 2 years of age should include in the daily diet.

Food Group	Recommended Servings (2,000 calorie diet)	Representative Foods
Grains	6 oz	Whole grain breads, cereals, rice, pasta 1 slice bread = 1 oz 1 cup cereal = 1 oz ½ cup cooked pasta = 1 oz
Vegetables	2 ½ cups (raw, cooked, or juice)	Broccoli, carrots, dry beans and peas, corn, potatoes, tomatoes
Fruits	2 cups	1 small banana, orange, ¼ cup dried apricots
Milk	3 cups (2 cups for children 2 to 8)	2% milk, yogurt, cheese
Meat & Beans	5 ½ oz	Beef, poultry, eggs, kidney beans, soy beans, fish, nuts and seeds, peanut butter 1 small chicken breast = 3 oz 1 egg = 1 oz ¼ cup dried cooked beans = 1 oz
Oils	6 tsp	Canola oil, corn oil, olive oil, nuts, olives, some fish

Δ   A person walking the steps of the pyramid is a reminder to balance calorie intake with suitable activity:

- Engage in **physical activity for 30 min most days** of the week.

- To prevent weight gain, 60 min of moderate intensity physical activity a day may be necessary.

- Children and teenagers should be physically active for 60 min/day.

Strategies for Weight Control

Δ   Assess **body mass index** (**BMI**) to determine an estimate of overall body fat. Normal BMI range is **18.5 to 24.9**. A BMI of 35 or more places an adult at increased risk for cardiovascular disease, hypertension, type 2 diabetes mellitus, and dyslipidemia.

Δ   A **physically fit person** has strength, flexibility, cardiopulmonary endurance, and muscular endurance.

Δ   Encourage increased physical activity as the first step to becoming physically fit and for the maintenance of energy balance. Although aerobic exercise burns more calories, 20 min of low- and moderate-intensity exercise burns more fat.

Δ   To lose 1 lb of body fat per week, an adult must have an energy deficit of 3,500 calories (500 cal/day).

Δ   **Adequate nutrition**, based on the Food Pyramid, maintains energy balance, and increased physical activity promotes and maintains weight loss.

Δ   Monitor progress toward a healthy lifestyle through a **daily log** of food intake and physical activity.

Strategies for Promotion of Specific Areas of Health

Δ   **Healthy Hearts**

- Limit saturated fat to 10% of calories and cholesterol to 300 mg/day.

- For individuals with elevated low density lipoproteins (LDL), the American Heart Association (AHA) recommends increasing monounsaturated fats and soluble fiber.

Δ   **Healthy Nervous Systems**

- Normal functioning of the nervous system depends on adequate levels of the B-complex vitamins, especially thiamin, niacin, and vitamins B_6 and B_{12}.

- Calcium and sodium are important regulators of nerve responses. Eating the recommended servings from the grain and dairy food groups provides these nutrients.

Δ **Healthy Bones**

- Including the recommended servings from the Food Pyramid's dairy group supplies the calcium, magnesium, and phosphorus necessary for bone formation and the vitamin D that aids in the absorption of calcium and phosphorus.

- Weight-bearing physical activity is also essential to decrease the risk of osteoporosis.

Δ **Good Bowel Function**

- Normal bowel functioning depends on adequate fluid intake and 25 g/day of fiber for women and 38 g/day for men.

- The minimum number of servings from the Food Pyramid's fruit, vegetable, and grain food groups (specifically whole grains) provides these essentials.

Δ **Cancer Prevention**

- A well-balanced diet, using the Food Pyramid, and a healthy weight are general guidelines to prevent cancer.

- Increase high-fiber plant-based foods.

- Limit saturated and polyunsaturated fat, while emphasizing foods with monounsaturated fat or omega-3 fatty acids, such as nuts and fish.

- Limit sodium intake.

- Avoid excess alcohol intake.

- Include regular exercise.

Nursing Assessments/Data Collection and Interventions

Δ Assess nutritional status and dietary intake patterns (see Chapter 1).

Δ Assess exercise and activity patterns.

Δ Identify appropriate nutrition standards to utilize as teaching tools.

Δ Assess energy balance using anthropometric data (see Chapter 1).

Primary Reference:

Dudek, S. G. (2006). *Nutrition essentials for nursing practice* (5th ed.). Philadelphia: Lippincott Williams & Wilkins.

Additional Resources:

For more information on the Food Guide Pyramid, visit the USDA's MyPyramid.gov at: *www.MyPyramid.gov*.

Chapter 4: Health Promotion

Application Exercises

Scenario: A nurse is discussing nutrition with a client who has a BMI of 34 and is receptive to health teaching. The client recorded the following menu for three breakfasts last week:

> 2 scrambled eggs
>
> 2 slices of bacon
>
> 1 slice of toast with butter
>
> ½ cup orange juice

1. What recommendations should be shared with this client in regard to the Dietary Guidelines for Americans?

2. What teaching should be provided concerning this BMI and physical activity?

3. To decrease risk factors for common health problems, a nurse should encourage an increased intake of which foods?

4. What is the recommended daily fat intake?

5. What is the recommended daily intake of salt?

6. Match the following:

   _____ Healthy heart   A. Calcium, vitamin D, and weight-bearing exercise

   _____ Healthy bones   B. Fluid, fiber, and exercise

   _____ Good bowel function   C. Limit saturated fat to 10% of total caloric intake

Chapter 4: Health Promotion

Application Exercises Answer Key

Scenario: A nurse is discussing nutrition with a client who has a BMI of 34 and is receptive to health teaching. The client recorded the following menu for three breakfasts last week:

2 scrambled eggs

2 slices of bacon

1 slice of toast with butter

½ cup orange juice

1. What recommendations should be shared with this client in regard to the Dietary Guidelines for Americans?

The client may need to reduce the saturated fat in the diet. Egg yolks, bacon, and butter are all high in saturated fat and cholesterol. The client did have high-quality protein (egg white) and 1 serving of fruit.

2. What teaching should be provided concerning this BMI and physical activity?

Normal BMI range is 18.5 to 24.9. The client is at risk for cardiovascular disease, hypertension, elevated triglycerides with a low concentration of high density lipoproteins, and diabetes. The client should start an exercise program that will include low- to moderate-intensity exercise each day, after consulting the primary care provider.

3. To decrease risk factors for common health problems, a nurse should encourage an increased intake of which foods?

High-fiber foods, such as fruits and vegetables, should be encouraged. The nurse should also encourage limiting saturated fat intake.

4. What is the recommended daily fat intake?

Fat intake should comprise 30% of total caloric intake, with less than 10% from saturated fat.

5. What is the recommended daily intake of salt?

Less than 2,300 mg/day.

6. Match the following:

    __C__ Healthy heart   A. Calcium, vitamin D, and weight-bearing exercise

    __A__ Healthy bones   B. Fluid, fiber, and exercise

    __B__ Good bowel function   C. Limit saturated fat to 10% of total caloric intake

Unit 1   Principles of Nutrition

Chapter 5:   Cultural Awareness: Food and Nutrition
                  Contributor: Marsha L. Ray, MSN, RN

⟳ NCLEX® Connections:

Learning Objective: Review and apply knowledge within "**Cultural Awareness: Food and Nutrition**" in readiness for performance of the following nutrition nursing activities as outlined by the NCLEX® test plans:

Δ   Assess/collect data regarding the importance of the client's culture/ethnicity when planning/providing/evaluating dietary interventions.

Δ   Demonstrate sensitivity to the client's cultural practices when providing or reinforcing dietary teaching.

📖 Key Points

Δ   **Cultural traditions impact food choices** and routines, and nurses should consider these implications when planning and communicating nutritional goals with clients.

Δ   **Acculturation** is the process of a cultural, ethnic, or religious group's adopting the dominant culture's behaviors, beliefs, and values.

Δ   Care must be taken by the nurse to avoid demonstrating **ethnocentrism**, which is the belief that one's own cultural practices are the only correct behaviors, beliefs, attitudes, and values.

Culture and Nutrition

Δ   The degree to which clients follow their cultural, ethnic, or religious group's traditional nutritional practices should guide the nurse's care.

Δ   The first generation members of a family are more likely to follow their **traditional foodway** (all aspects of an individual's nutritional practices), with subsequent generations incorporating the host culture's food practices through socialization with the host culture.

Δ   Frequently, the dominant culture's breakfast and lunch foods are eaten, and **traditional meals** are consumed at dinner and at symbolic events (religious holidays, weddings, and childbirth).

Δ   To avoid ethnocentrism, nurses should understand that ideas regarding food choices and nutrition vary among cultures. For instance:

  • Beetles and bugs are food items in some cultures.

  • Not all cultures identify with the American ideal of slimness.

  • Milk is not a good source of calcium in many cultures (especially when compared to the Euro-American foodway) due to the **high incidence of lactose intolerance** in those cultural groups.

Δ   **Culturally respectful communication** is necessary in all forms of client communication, including client education on nutrition.

  • The appropriateness of **eye contact** and **touch** vary among cultures and can impact communication. Orientation to time and literacy also impact communication.

  • Language barriers can be overcome utilizing agency-approved medical **translators**.

  • Instructions written in the client's language convey respect and improve care.

Δ   **Americanization** of traditional foodways may have positive or negative consequences.

  • New foods are added to the traditional diet.

  • Food dishes are made in new ways.

  • Cuisine items may be deleted entirely.

Δ   **Religion** has a profound influence on foodways, especially since religion crosses geographic boundaries. Implications include:

  • Feasting/celebration foods.

  • **Special food preparations**, such as kosher kitchens in Orthodox Jewish homes.

  • **Prescriptive guidelines** for animal slaughter, as in Islam and Orthodox Judaism.

  • **Avoidance of stimulants** like coffee, tea, and caffeinated soda by Muslims and Mormons.

  • The practice of **vegetarianism** by Seventh-Day Adventists and some Buddhists.

  • **Fasting** for some religious holidays, such as Ramadan for Muslims, or refraining from meat consumption on Ash Wednesday and Fridays during Lent for Catholics.

Δ Changes in the American foodway reflect **cultural changes in American society** and present nutritional challenges. Some trends that have made a significant impact on nutrition include:

- Make it quick; time is in short supply.

- Make it easy; add only three to four ingredients or pop it ready-made in the microwave.

- When all else fails, go to the **drive-thru** or **order/eat out**.

Δ Paying careful attention to **reading labels**, adding **beneficial side dishes**, practicing **portion control**, and **choosing better dine-out choices** can minimize the detrimental effect of these societal changes that otherwise result in diets that are high in salt, carbohydrates, fat, refined sugars, and caffeine while providing low amounts of fiber and calcium.

Meeting Nutritional Needs with a Vegetarian Diet

Δ Individuals following a **pure vegetarian** diet do not consume animal products of any type, including eggs and all milk products. In general, these diets are adequate in protein due to intake of nuts and legumes, such as dried peas and cooked beans. Vitamin B_{12} and vitamin D supplementation may be needed with a pure **vegan** diet.

Δ Individuals following a **lactovegetarian** diet consume milk products in addition to vegetables. Individuals following a **lacto-ovo-vegetarian** diet consume milk products and eggs in addition to vegetables.

Selected U.S. Cultural Subgroups

Δ **African American** ("Soul Food"): origins in the Caribbean, Central America, East Africa, and West Africa

- Traditional Foods

  ◊ Rice, grits, cornbread; hominy, okra, greens, sweet potatoes; apples, peaches; buttermilk, pudding, Cheddar or American cheese; ham, pork, chicken, catfish, black-eyed peas, red and pinto beans, peanuts; soft drinks, fatback, chitterlings, banana pudding

- Traditional Food Preparation

  ◊ Frying and cooking with added animal fats (lard, salt pork)

  ◊ Promoting a shared inheritance and loving family

- Acculturation

  ◊ Increased milk consumption

  ◊ Use of packaged meat, pork preferred

  ◊ Continued low intake of fruit and vegetables

- Nutritional Health Risks
  ◊ High in fat, protein, and sodium, and low in potassium, calcium, and fiber
  ◊ Low fresh fruit and vegetable intake
  ◊ Substantial weight ("having meat on your bones") equated with good health and prosperity
  ◊ Increased incidence of type 2 diabetes mellitus and hypertension
- Health Promotion
  ◊ Encourage frying lightly with canola/olive oil instead of in animal fats.
  ◊ Introduce fresh fruit and vegetable dishes and decrease meat portions.
  ◊ Suggest dark green leafy vegetables and low-fat cheeses as calcium sources.
  ◊ Associate "good health" with better food choices and portion control.
  ◊ Advise preparing unhealthy soul food items only at special occasions.

Δ **Asian American** ("Chinese Food"): origins in the Far East, Southeast Asia, and the Indian subcontinent

- Traditional Foods
  ◊ Wheat (northern), rice (southern), noodles; fruits, land and sea vegetables, nuts/seeds, soy foods (tofu), nut/seed oils; fish, shellfish, poultry, eggs; sweets; rarely red meats; tea, beer
- Traditional Food Preparation
  ◊ Fruits and vegetables peeled and raw
  ◊ Stir-frying in oils quickly to retain crispness of vegetables
  ◊ Cutting meat and poultry into bite-sized pieces
  ◊ Cooking with salt, oil, and oil products (spices important)
  ◊ Preventing "imbalances" and indigestion through balance of yin and yang
- Acculturation
  ◊ Increased use of bread and cereal; rice/wheat staple remains high
  ◊ Utilization of new location's fruit and vegetables with increased use of fruit and salads
  ◊ Increased use of sugar through soft drinks, candy, and desserts
- Nutritional Health Risks
  ◊ High sodium intake
  ◊ Increased cancer rate as living in the U.S. continues

- Health Promotion
  ◊ Encourage continued use of plant-based diet and food preparation as the generations take on "American foods."
  ◊ Moderate salt intake.
  ◊ Limit sugar-laden foods.

Δ **Latino American** ("Mexican Food"): origins in Mexico, Caribbean, and Central and South America

- Traditional Foods
  ◊ Rice, maize, tortillas; tropical fruits, vegetables; nuts, beans, legumes; eggs, cheese, seafood, poultry; infrequent sweets and red meat

- Traditional Food Preparation
  ◊ Frying and stewing in lard or oil
  ◊ Meats ground or chopped
  ◊ Meat mixed with vegetables & grains or stuffed (tamales)
  ◊ Heavily spiced with common use of chilies
  ◊ Minimal use of sugar
  ◊ "Hot" and "cold" food choices maintain "balance"

- Acculturation
  ◊ Increased milk use
  ◊ Decreased meat consumption as mixed meals decline
  ◊ Replacement of maize by wheat in tortillas and breads
  ◊ Decreased bean use and change in rice preparation to plain boiled rice
  ◊ Increased fruit and vegetable intake
  ◊ Added fats in the form of butter or salad dressings on cooked vegetables and side salads
  ◊ Replacement of fruit-based drinks by sugar-laden drinks

- Nutritional Health Risks
  ◊ Increased incidence of type 2 diabetes mellitus
  ◊ Positive associations with substantial weight

- Health Promotion
  ◊ Encourage boiling, braising, and baking in place of frying and stewing in lard and oils.
  ◊ Return to traditional corn tortillas.
  ◊ Encourage use of fresh unprocessed/preserved plant-based diet.

Primary Reference:

Dudek, S. G. (2006). *Nutrition essentials for nursing practice* (5th ed.). Philadelphia: Lippincott Williams & Wilkins.

Additional Resources:

Lutz, C. A., & Przytulski, K. R. (2006). *Nutrition and diet therapy: Evidence-based applications* (4th ed.). Philadelphia: F.A. Davis Company.

Purnell, L. D., & Paulanka, B. J. (2005). *Guide to culturally competent health care.* Philadelphia: F.A. Davis Company.

Chapter 5: Cultural Awareness

Application Exercises

Scenario: A nurse is caring for a 53-year-old client recently admitted to a cardiac telemetry unit post myocardial infarction. The client is a business executive who is Euro-American. He states that he doesn't understand why he had a heart attack, and says, "I've been eating like my Asian co-workers in China, and they are so healthy." When asked how he prepares his Asian cuisine, he states that during the work week he eats a bowl of multigrain cereal for breakfast and often eats at one of several local Asian restaurants or gets Chinese take-out for lunch and dinner.

1. Discuss the traditional Asian foodway and the benefits of this dietary pattern on the heart.

2. Describe the steps that should be taken to determine the benefits and risks of this client's eating pattern.

3. Describe the major teaching points that should be on the nutritional teaching plan for this client.

4. Identify the healthy and unhealthy aspects of the following traditional foodways:

Traditional Foodway	Healthy Aspects	Unhealthy Aspects
African American		
Asian American		
Latino American		

5. An ethnocentric approach to filling out a client's menu to provide for more calcium is to

    A. ask the client what he likes to eat.

    B. call the dietician to fill the menu out.

    C. recommend one's own favorite foods.

    D. have the family fill out the menu.

6. A client whose foodway is vegetarian requests a mid-afternoon snack. Which of the following should the nurse provide for the client?

> A. Several wheat crackers and a boiled egg
>
> B. Custard cup and a cup of coffee
>
> C. An apple and a slice of cheese
>
> D. Fruit juice and mixed nuts

7. The greatest impact on a second-generation immigrant's traditional dietary patterns is the

> A. fast pace of the American society.
>
> B. inability to obtain traditional foods in this host country.
>
> C. adoption of the American foodway.
>
> D. wide variety of "ethnic" foods in the United States.

8. Which of the following statements made by a nurse in a class on culture and food is **inaccurate**?

> A. "Clients who practice Roman Catholicism do not drink coffee, tea, or caffeinated sodas."
>
> B. "By working closely with nutritional services, I can meet the prescribed diet and still follow my client's religious practices."
>
> C. "Clients who follow the teachings of Islam and Orthodox Judaism need to eat only specified animals that are slaughtered under strict guidelines."
>
> D. "Because not all individuals in one country necessarily practice the same religion, I cannot consider ethnicity alone in my plan of care."

Chapter 5: Cultural Awareness

Application Exercises Answer Key

Scenario: A nurse is caring for a 53-year-old client recently admitted to a cardiac telemetry unit post myocardial infarction. The client is a business executive who is Euro-American. He states that he doesn't understand why he had a heart attack, and says, "I've been eating like my Asian co-workers in China, and they are so healthy." When asked how he prepares his Asian cuisine, he states that during the work week he eats a bowl of multigrain cereal for breakfast and often eats at one of several local Asian restaurants or gets Chinese take-out for lunch and dinner.

1. Discuss the traditional Asian foodway and the benefits of this dietary pattern on the heart.

  Traditional Asian foodway:

    Δ **Plant-based diet**

    Δ **Consume raw fruits and vegetables**

    Δ **Stir-fry quickly to retain crispness of foods, which retain vitamins**

    Δ **Use of plant-based oils**

    Δ **High sodium content of diet from spices and condiments (soy source)**

    Δ **Major protein sources are plant-based (soy), fish, shellfish, poultry, and nuts**

    Δ **Rare use of red meats, consumed in small portions**

    Δ **Moderate portions of all food groups (cultural value on moderation in life)**

  Benefits to heart:

    Δ **Low cholesterol and lipids**

    Δ **Generally not overweight**

2. Describe the steps that should be taken to determine the benefits and risks of this client's eating pattern.

    Δ **Assess your knowledge of the foodway and obtain assistance if necessary.**

    Δ **Set an unhurried and attentive atmosphere for a discussion.**

    Δ **Ask the client to describe 2 days of typical meals, snacks, and fluid consumption during his work week.**

Δ   Discuss how the meals and snacks are prepared.

Δ   Discuss the portions/amounts of the different foods typically consumed.

Δ   Supply written material on traditional Asian foods, food preparations, and portions.

Δ   Compare and contrast the traditional Asian foodway with the client's description of his diet.

Δ   Explore ways to more closely align the client's diet with the traditional Asian foodway.

Δ   Request a dietary consult from the provider.

Δ   Provide printed follow-up information from discussion.

3. Describe the major teaching points that should be on the nutritional teaching plan for this client.

Encourage continued high intake of a plant-based diet, decreased salt intake, and adequate calcium intake.

4. Identify the healthy and unhealthy aspects of the following traditional foodways:

Traditional Foodway	Healthy Aspects	Unhealthy Aspects
African American	Family involvement	Animal proteins and oils Increased sodium Increased incidence of type 2 diabetes mellitus
Asian American	Plant-based diet Fruits in diet	Increased sodium Risk calcium deficit due to plant base
Latino American	Plant-based diet Fruits in diet Family involvement	Animal proteins and oils Increased incidence of type 2 diabetes mellitus Risk calcium deficit due to lactose intolerance

5. An ethnocentric approach to filling out a client's menu to provide for more calcium is to

    A. ask the client what he likes to eat.

    B. call the dietician to fill the menu out.

    C. recommend one's own favorite foods.

    D. have the family fill out the menu.

Answer "C" is an example of an ethnocentric approach. Ethnocentrism is the belief that the dominant or host culture's practices are the only correct behaviors/beliefs.

6. A client whose foodway is vegetarian requests a mid-afternoon snack. Which of the following should the nurse provide for the client?

      A. Several wheat crackers and a boiled egg

      B. Custard cup and a cup of coffee

      C. An apple and a slice of cheese

      D. Fruit juice and mixed nuts

Answer "D" is the only combination that is vegetarian. Without further assessment of exactly what the client means by "vegetarian," the nurse cannot know if the client follows a vegan foodway or a foodway that is predominately plant-based with the addition of other foods like eggs, milk, and milk products (which is classified as lacto-ovo-vegetarian).

7. The greatest impact on a second-generation immigrant's traditional dietary patterns is the

      A. fast pace of the American society.

      B. inability to obtain traditional foods in this host country.

      C. adoption of the American foodway.

      D. wide variety of "ethnic" foods in the United States.

Foodway is defined as all aspects of an individual's nutritional practices (what is food, food sources, inclusion of family into food planning and preparation, timing and number of meals, food preparation, food symbolism).

8. Which of the following statements made by a nurse in a class on culture and food is **inaccurate**?

      A. "Clients who practice Roman Catholicism do not drink coffee, tea, or caffeinated sodas."

      B. "By working closely with nutritional services, I can meet the prescribed diet and still follow my client's religious practices."

      C. "Clients who follow the teachings of Islam and Orthodox Judaism need to eat only specified animals that are slaughtered under strict guidelines."

      D. "Because not all individuals in one country necessarily practice the same religion, I cannot consider ethnicity alone in my plan of care."

Answer "A" is the only answer containing incorrect information. Stimulants such as coffee, tea, or caffeinated sodas are not consumed by Muslims or Mormons. A Roman Catholic cultural practice is not eating meat on Ash Wednesday or Fridays during Lent.

Unit 1   Principles of Nutrition

Chapter 6:   Food Safety and Food-Medication Interactions

Contributor: Dana Bartlett, MSN, RN, CSPI

NCLEX® Connections:

Learning Objective: Review and apply knowledge within "**Food Safety and Food-Medication Interactions**" in readiness for performance of the following nutrition nursing activities as outlined by the NCLEX® test plans:

Δ   Assess/collect data regarding the client's ability to eat.

Δ   Inform staff and the client/family/significant other of appropriate infection control procedures.

Δ   Assess/monitor the client for potential/actual interactions between food and medications.

Key Points

Food Safety

Δ   Ingestion of food poses a **risk of aspiration** in some circumstances. To minimize the risk of aspiration with food intake, food should only be consumed by individuals who are conscious and have an intact gag or swallow reflex. For clients with a known risk for aspiration (for example, following a stroke or a procedure involving anesthesia of the esophagus), it is important for the nurse to check the client's ability to swallow prior to eating.

Δ   Food safety requires:

•   Proper food storage.

•   Proper handling.

•   Proper preparation guidelines.

Δ   **Proper food storage** guidelines include:

•   **Fresh meat:** 1 to 2 days at 40° F or cooler.

•   **Fish:** 1 to 2 days at 40° F or cooler.

- **Dairy products:** Store in the refrigerator for 5 days for milk and 3 to 4 weeks for cheese.

- **Eggs:** Store in the refrigerator for 3 weeks for fresh in shell and 1 week for hard-boiled.

- **Fruits and vegetables:** Keep for 3 to 5 days; citrus fruits and apples, 1 week or longer.

- **Pantry items:** Store in a dry, dark place at room temperature.

- **Canned goods:** Store 1 year or longer at room temperature.

Δ **Proper handling** is relatively simple:

- Wash hands and surfaces frequently.

- Separate foods to avoid cross-contamination.

Δ **Proper preparation** guidelines include:

- Cook food to the proper temperature (roasts and steaks, 145° F; chicken, 180° F; ground beef, 160° F).

- Products that contain eggs must be cooked to 160° F.

Δ It is important to understand **packaging labels**:

- **Sell-by date** is the last recommended day of sale.

- **Use-by date** tells you for how long the product will maintain top quality.

- **Expiration date** is the last day the product should be used or consumed.

Food-Medication Interactions

Δ Foods and medications can interact in the body in ways that alter the intended action of those medications. Both the composition and timing of food intake should be considered in relation to medication use.

Δ Foods can alter the absorption of medications:

- **Decreased absorption**: Food can decrease the *rate* of absorption and also the *extent* of absorption.
    - ◊ Reducing the **rate** of absorption alters only the *onset* of peak effects
    - ◊ Reducing the **extent** of absorption **reduces the intended effect** of the medication.

Δ Some medications cause **gastric irritation**. It is important to **take certain medications with food** to avoid gastric upset. Examples include ibuprofen (Advil, Motrin), some antibiotics like amoxicillin, and some anti-depressants like bupropion (Wellbutrin).

Δ   Certain foods **alter the metabolism/actions** of medications:

- **Grapefruit juice** interferes with the metabolism of many medications resulting in an increased serum level of the medication.

- Consumption of **foods high in vitamin K** (green leafy vegetables, eggs, liver) can decrease the anticoagulant effects of warfarin (Coumadin).

- **Foods high in protein, amino acids, and vitamin B$_6$** can all increase the metabolism of the anti-Parkinson's medication levodopa (L-dopa, Sinemet), which decreases the duration of its therapeutic effects.

- **Licorice** can cause hyperkalemia (elevated serum potassium). Excess ingestion can be dangerous for clients taking digoxin (Lanoxin), stimulant laxatives, some beta-blockers, ACE inhibitors, some calcium channel blockers, MAO inhibitors, and spironolactone.

- **Tyramine** is a naturally occurring amine that is found in many foods and has **hypertensive effects** similar to other amines, such as norepinephrine. Tyramine is metabolized by monoamine oxidase (MAO), and clients taking an MAO inhibitor who eat food high in tyramine may suffer a hypertensive crisis. Foods high in tyramine include aged mature cheese, smoked meats, red wines, and pickled meats.

Nursing Assessments/Data Collection and Interventions

Δ   Nursing assessments should include a complete dietary profile of the client, medications, baseline knowledge about food safety, and medication and food interactions.

Δ   Nursing interventions should include basic teaching about food safety and teaching about the interactions between foods and the client's medications.

Primary Reference:

Dudek, S. G. (2006). *Nutrition essentials for nursing practice* (5th ed.). Philadelphia: Lippincott Williams & Wilkins.

Additional Resources:

Lehne, R. A. (2004). *Pharmacology for nursing care* (5th ed.). St. Louis, MO: W.B. Saunders Company.

Chapter 6: Food Safety and Food-Medication Interactions

Application Exercises

Scenario: A client recently had visitors who brought a gift basket containing a bottle of red wine and cheese as a gift. One hour after the visitors left, the client reports a headache. After reviewing the client's prescribed medications, the nurse notes that the client is currently taking isocarboxazid (Marplan), an MAO inhibitor.

1. What is a possible explanation for the client's reported headache?

2. How should the nurse explain this situation to the client and what type of dietary counseling is indicated?

Scenario: A nurse is caring for a client who has just begun taking warfarin (Coumadin) for its anticoagulant effects.

3. Foods high in what fat-soluble vitamin can decrease the anticoagulant effects of warfarin (Coumadin)?

4. Which of the following are appropriate food choices for this client? (Check all that apply.)

_____ Peanut butter sandwich and orange juice

_____ Leaf lettuce salad

_____ Hamburger and French fries

_____ Carrots and salad dressing

_____ Steamed broccoli

_____ Crackers with cheese

_____ Omelet

5. The client states he does not like the hospital food and asks if his family can bring in food. What teaching should the nurse provide to the client and his family regarding the types of food that are appropriate?

6. The juice of what citrus fruit can interfere with the metabolism of many medications? What is the result on medication levels?

7. Why are high amounts of protein, vitamin B$_6$, and amino acids not recommended for clients taking the anti-Parkinson's medication levodopa (L-dopa, Sinemet)?

8. A client just picked up her new amoxicillin prescription at her local pharmacy. What instructions might the nurse expect to see on the label and why?

9. **True or False:** Dairy products such as cheese and milk can be stored safely for up to 3 months as long as they are refrigerated.

10. **True or False:** Ground beef and products containing eggs must be cooked to a minimum of 160° F.

11. **True or False:** Use-by date represents the date by which a product must be discarded.

Chapter 6: Food Safety and Food-Medication Interactions

Application Exercises Answer Key

Scenario: A client recently had visitors who brought a gift basket containing a bottle of red wine and cheese as a gift. One hour after the visitors left, the client reports a headache. After reviewing the client's prescribed medications, the nurse notes that the client is currently taking isocarboxazid (Marplan), an MAO inhibitor.

1. What is a possible explanation for the client's reported headache?

> **Cheese and wine are two foods that contain tyramine, an amine that has hypertensive effects. Tyramine is metabolized by monoamine oxidase (MAO). Clients taking MAO inhibitors may experience a hypertensive crisis because the medication impedes the metabolism of tyramine. Headaches are one symptom of a hypertensive crisis.**

2. How should the nurse explain this situation to the client and what type of dietary counseling is indicated?

> **The nurse should explain that tyramine is a natural component of some foods. If it is not metabolized, it can elevate blood pressure. The nurse should also provide the client with a list of foods that are naturally high in tyramine. Examples of foods high in tyramine include smoked meats, aged cheeses, and red wines.**

Scenario: A nurse is caring for a client who has just begun taking warfarin (Coumadin) for its anticoagulant effects.

3. Foods high in what fat-soluble vitamin can decrease the anticoagulant effects of warfarin (Coumadin)?

> **Vitamin K**

4. Which of the following are appropriate food choices for this client? (Check all that apply.)

    __X__ Peanut butter sandwich and orange juice

    _____ Leaf lettuce salad

    __X__ Hamburger and French fries

    __X__ Carrots and salad dressing

    _____ Steamed broccoli

    __X__ Crackers with cheese

    _____ Omelet

5. The client states he does not like the hospital food and asks if his family can bring in food. What teaching should the nurse provide to the client and his family regarding the types of food that are appropriate?

The nurse should encourage the client to maintain consistent vitamin K intake. Additionally, the nurse should provide the client and family with a list of foods that are high in vitamin K. It should include green leafy vegetables, liver, eggs, and milk.

6. The juice of what citrus fruit can interfere with the metabolism of many medications? What is the result on medication levels?

Grapefruit juice interferes with the metabolism of many medications, resulting in increased serum levels of medications.

7. Why are high amounts of protein, vitamin B$_6$, and amino acids not recommended for clients taking the anti-Parkinson's medication levodopa (L-dopa, Sinemet)?

Foods high in protein, vitamin B$_6$, and amino acids increase the metabolism of levodopa, thus decreasing the duration of its therapeutic effects.

8. A client just picked up her new amoxicillin prescription at her local pharmacy. What instructions might the nurse expect to see on the label and why?

The nurse could expect the label to instruct the client to take the medication with food to avoid gastrointestinal upset.

9. **True or False:** Dairy products such as cheese and milk can be stored safely for up to 3 months as long as they are refrigerated.

False: Milk should be kept refrigerated for up to 5 days while cheese may be kept up to 3 to 4 weeks with proper refrigeration (40° F or below).

10. **True or False:** Ground beef and products containing eggs must be cooked to a minimum of 160° F.

True

11. **True or False:** Use-by date represents the date by which a product must be discarded.

False: The use-by date represents the date through which the product will maintain its highest quality. The expiration date represents the date by which the food item must be discarded.

Unit 2   Nutrition Across the Lifespan

Chapter 7:   Nutrition in Pregnancy and Lactation
Contributor: Dana Bartlett, MSN, RN, CSPI

NCLEX® Connections:

Learning Objective: Review and apply knowledge within "**Nutrition in Pregnancy and Lactation**" in readiness for performance of the following nutrition nursing activities as outlined by the NCLEX® test plans:

Δ   Evaluate the impact of pregnancy on the nutritional status and needs of the client.

Δ   Monitor the hydration status of the client during pregnancy and lactation.

Δ   Monitor the client's weight throughout pregnancy in relationship to nutritional goals.

Δ   Provide information to the client regarding appropriate dietary modifications for pregnancy and lactation.

Key Points

Δ   Good nutrition during pregnancy is essential for the health of the unborn child.

Δ   **Maternal nutritional demands are increased** for the development of the placenta, enlargement of the uterus, formation of amniotic fluid, increase in blood volume, and preparation of the breasts for lactation.

Δ   **Energy requirements** during pregnancy **increase** by approximately **15%**. Based on a 2,000 cal/day diet, women who become pregnant should consume an additional 300 cal/day to meet that requirement.

Δ   The nutritional requirements of women who are pregnant or lactating involve more than just increased caloric intake. Specific dietary **requirements for** both the **major nutrients** and **micronutrients** should be taught.

Dietary Guidelines During Pregnancy and Lactation

Δ   Achieving an appropriate amount of **weight gain** during pregnancy prepares a woman for the energy demands of labor and lactation, and it contributes to the delivery of a normal-birth-weight neonate.

Δ   The **recommended weight gain** during pregnancy varies for each woman, depending on her body mass index (BMI) and weight prior to pregnancy.

- Recommended weight gain during the **first trimester is 2 to 4 lb.**

- **Trimesters 2 and 3:**

  ◊ Normal weight – 1 lb/week for a total of 25 to 35 lb.

  ◊ Underweight – just more than 1 lb/week for a total of 28 to 40 lb.

  ◊ Overweight – 0.66 lb/week for a total of 15 to 25 lb.

Δ   Lactating women require an **increase** in their **daily caloric intake**. The amount required will vary based on the amount of weight gained during pregnancy. For women who gained the recommended amount of weight, the recommendation is an **additional 500 cal/day**.

Major and Micronutrient Requirements During Pregnancy and Lactation

Δ   Dietary requirements for the major nutrients include:

- **Protein** should comprise **20% of the daily total calorie intake.** The recommended daily allowance (RDA) for protein during pregnancy is 1.1 g/kg/day. Protein is essential for the rapid tissue growth of maternal and fetal structures, amniotic fluid, and the extra blood volume. Women who are pregnant should be aware that animal sources of protein might also contain large amounts of fats.

- **Fat**, as usual, should be **limited to 30%** of total daily calorie intake.

- **Carbohydrates** should comprise **50% of the total daily calorie intake**. Ensuring adequate carbohydrate intake allows for protein to be spared and available for the synthesis of fetal tissue.

Δ   The need for most **vitamins and minerals** increases during pregnancy and lactation. Vitamins are essential for the formation of blood, the absorption of iron, and the development of fetal tissue. The following table lists the comparative RDAs of major vitamins for women age 19 to 30 during nonpregnancy, pregnancy, and lactation.

Nutrient	Nonpregnant	Pregnant	Lactating
Protein (g)	46	71	71
Vitamin A (μg)	700	770	1,300
Vitamin C (mg)	75	85	120
Vitamin D (μg)*	5	5	5
Vitamin E (μg)	15	15	19
Vitamin K (μg)*	90	90	90
Thiamin (mg)	1.1	1.4	1.4

Nutrient	Nonpregnant	Pregnant	Lactating
Riboflavin (mg)	1.1	1.4	1.6
Niacin (mg)	14	18	17
Vitamin B_6 (mg)	1.3	1.9	2.0
Folate (µg)	400	600	500
Vitamin B_{12} (µg)	2.4	2.6	2.8
Pantothenic acid (mg)*	5	6	7
Biotin (µg)*	30	30	35
Choline (mg)*	425	450	550
Calcium (mg)*	1,000	1,000	1,000
Iron (mg)	18	27	9
Magnesium (mg)	310	350	310
Selenium (µg)	55	60	70
Zinc (mg)	8	11	12

*Values represent adequate intakes (AIs).

Source: Food and Nutrition Information Center. *Dietary Reference Intakes (DRI) and Recommended Dietary Allowances (RDA)*. Retrieved May 4, 2006, from www.nal.usda.gov/fnic/etext/000105.html

Additional Dietary Recommendations

Δ **Fluid:** Drink **8 to 10 glasses (8 oz)** of fluids every day. Preferable fluids include water, fruit juice, or milk. Carbonated beverages and fruit drinks provide few or no nutrients.

Δ **Alcohol:** It is recommended that women abstain from alcohol consumption during pregnancy.

Δ **Caffeine:** Caffeine crosses the placenta and can affect the movements and heart rate of the fetus. However, moderate use **(less than 300 mg/day)** does not appear to be harmful.

Δ **Vegetarian diets:** Well-balanced vegetarian diets that include dairy products can provide all the nutritional requirements of pregnancy.

Δ **Folic acid intake** should not be neglected. It is necessary for the neurological development of the fetus, and it prevents birth defects.

Δ **Iron** can be obtained from dairy products and meats, especially red meats. Consuming foods high in **vitamin C** aids the absorption of iron.

Dietary Complications During Pregnancy

Δ **Nausea** and **constipation** are common during pregnancy.

- For nausea, try dry crackers or toast. Avoid alcohol, caffeine, fats, and spices. Also avoid drinking fluids with meals, and **DO NOT take a medication to control nausea** without first checking with the primary care provider.

- For constipation, increase fluid consumption and include extra fiber in the diet. Fruits, vegetables, and whole grains all contain fiber.

Nursing Assessments/Data Collection and Interventions

Δ Nursing assessments should include a complete profile of the client's knowledge base regarding nutritional requirements during pregnancy.

Δ Additionally, the nurse should review the appropriate and recommended dietary practices for pregnant and lactating women with the client, while also providing her with materials containing this information.

Primary Reference:

Dudek, S. G. (2006). *Nutrition essentials for nursing practice* (5th ed.). Philadelphia: Lippincott Williams & Wilkins.

Chapter 7: Nutrition in Pregnancy and Lactation

Application Exercises

Scenario: A nurse is caring for a client who is 6 weeks pregnant. This is her initial visit to the primary care provider's office.

1. The client is concerned that she will gain too much weight during the pregnancy, and she states that she is going to really watch what she eats. The client's BMI and current weight indicate that she falls within the normal range. How much weight should this client expect to gain?

2. The nurse provides the client with guidelines for her major nutrient intake. Match the appropriate percentage of caloric intake with its corresponding nutrient.

    _____ Fat   A. 50%

    _____ Protein   B. 30%

    _____ Carbohydrates   C. 20%

3. Explain why obtaining adequate carbohydrate intake is important for expectant and lactating mothers.

4. What mineral is commonly prescribed in low doses for newly expectant mothers? List three examples of foods that are good sources of this mineral.

Scenario: A nurse is caring for a mother who is breastfeeding. The mother states that she is glad to see that she is regaining her pre-pregnancy appearance. She also states that the baby seems hungry all the time. The nurse notes that the baby's weight has not changed significantly since her last visit 2 weeks ago.

5. What information is important to share with this client?

6. **True or False:** The daily caloric intake requirements for a lactating mother are less than those of an expectant mother.

7. The client asks which foods are high in protein and would be appropriate for her to eat. Select proper food choices from the list below. (Check all that apply.)

    _____ Chocolate bar

    _____ Milkshake

    _____ Yogurt parfait with granola and strawberries

    _____ Turkey sandwich with lettuce

    _____ Celery stalks with peanut butter

    _____ Lemonade and saltine crackers

Scenario: A woman who is 7 weeks pregnant states that she is experiencing nausea each morning when she wakes.

---

8. What actions should the nurse encourage the client to take?

9. **True or False:** The nurse should recommend that the client obtain an over-the-counter nausea medication if the symptoms persist.

---

10. What information should a nurse share with a client who is pregnant regarding management of constipation?

11. Why is folate (folic acid) an important nutrient during pregnancy?

12. How much fluid does a pregnant woman need each day, and what are recommended sources of fluids?

Chapter 7: Nutrition in Pregnancy and Lactation

Application Exercises Answer Key

Scenario: A nurse is caring for a client who is 6 weeks pregnant. This is her initial visit to the primary care provider's office.

1. The client is concerned that she will gain too much weight during the pregnancy, and she states that she is going to really watch what she eats. The client's BMI and current weight indicate that she falls within the normal range. How much weight should this client expect to gain?

   The nurse should explain to the client that good nutrition during pregnancy is essential to the health of the fetus and that maternal nutritional demands are increased for the development of the placenta, amniotic fluid, increased blood volume, and preparation of the breasts for lactation. The nurse should also explain that the expected weight gain during the first trimester is 2 to 4 lb and that a woman of normal weight should expect to gain 1 lb/week during the second and third trimesters for a total of 25 to 35 lb.

2. The nurse provides the client with guidelines for her major nutrient intake. Match the appropriate percentage of caloric intake with its corresponding nutrient.

__B__ Fat	A. 50%
__C__ Protein	B. 30%
__A__ Carbohydrates	C. 20%

3. Explain why obtaining adequate carbohydrate intake is important for expectant and lactating mothers.

   Obtaining adequate carbohydrate intake is important to provide energy to the mother. This allows protein to be utilized for the development of fetal tissue.

4. What mineral is commonly prescribed in low doses for newly expectant mothers? List three examples of foods that are good sources of this mineral.

   Iron. Milk, cheese, and beef are good sources of iron.

Scenario: A nurse is caring for a mother who is breastfeeding. The mother states that she is glad to see that she is regaining her pre-pregnancy appearance. She also states that the baby seems hungry all the time. The nurse notes that the baby's weight has not changed significantly since her last visit 2 weeks ago.

5. What information is important to share with this client?

The nurse should inform the client that lactating women require an increase in their daily caloric intake. For a woman who gained the recommended amount of weight during pregnancy, an additional 500 cal/day is recommended.

6. **True or False:** The daily caloric intake requirements for a lactating mother are less than those of an expectant mother.

False: Pregnant women require an additional 300 cal/day, and lactating women require an additional 500 cal/day.

7. The client asks which foods are high in protein and would be appropriate for her to eat. Select proper food choices from the list below. (Check all that apply.)

_____ Chocolate bar

__X__ Milkshake

__X__ Yogurt parfait with granola and strawberries

__X__ Turkey sandwich with lettuce

__X__ Celery stalks with peanut butter

_____ Lemonade and saltine crackers

Scenario: A woman who is 7 weeks pregnant states that she is experiencing nausea each morning when she wakes.

8. What actions should the nurse encourage the client to take?

The nurse should first explain that nausea is a common issue during pregnancy. Encourage the client to eat bland foods such as toast, dry cereal, or crackers and to avoid consuming liquids with meals. Explain that avoiding alcohol, caffeine, and foods that are spicy or high in fat may help as well.

9. **True or False:** The nurse should recommend that the client obtain an over-the-counter nausea medication if the symptoms persist.

   False: A pregnant woman should NEVER take a medication before consulting with her primary care provider.

10. What information should a nurse share with a client who is pregnant regarding management of constipation?

   The nurse should tell the client that consuming a diet with extra fiber (fruits, vegetables, whole grains) and increasing fluid consumption may help to prevent or alleviate symptoms of constipation.

11. Why is folate (folic acid) an important nutrient during pregnancy?

   Folic acid is essential for the neurological development of the fetus, and it helps to prevent birth defects.

12. How much fluid does a pregnant woman need each day, and what are recommended sources of fluids?

   A woman should drink 8 to 10 glasses (8 oz) of fluids each day. Water, fruit juices, and milk are examples of nutritionally sound choices.

Unit 2   Nutrition Across the Lifespan

Chapter 8:   **Nutrition for Infants**

Contributor: Kathleen Jones, MEd, RN

NCLEX® Connections:

Learning Objective: Review and apply knowledge regarding **"Nutrition for Infants"** in readiness for performance of the following nutrition nursing activities as outlined by the NCLEX® test plans:

Δ   Recognize and report the client's deviations from growth and development norms.

Δ   Provide nutritional care appropriate to the developmental level of the client.

Key Points

Δ   **Growth rate** during infancy is more rapid than during any other period of the life cycle. It's important to understand normal growth patterns to determine the adequacy of an infant's nutritional intake.

Δ   **Birthweight** doubles by 4 to 6 months and triples by 1 year of age. The need for calories and nutrients is high to support the rapid rate of growth.

Δ   Appropriate **weight gain** averages 5 to 7 oz per week during the first 5 to 6 months and 4 to 5 oz per week from 6 to 12 months.

Δ   **Length** increases, on average, by 2.5 cm (1 in) per month during the first 6 months. The rate slows during the second 6 months. By 1 year, the birth length has increased by 50%.

Δ   **Head circumference** increases rapidly during the first 6 months at a rate of 1.5 cm (0.6 in) per month. The rate slows to 0.5 cm per month for months 6 to 12. By 1 year, head size should have increased by 33%. This is reflective of the growth of the nervous system.

Δ   Breast milk, infant formula, or a combination of the two is the sole source of nutrition for the first 4 to 6 months of life.

Δ   **Semi-solid foods** should not be introduced before 4 months of age to coincide with the development of head control, the ability to sit, and the back-and-forth motion of the tongue.

Δ   **Iron-fortified infant cereal** is the **first solid food** introduced because gestational iron stores begin to become depleted around 4 months of age.

Δ   **Cow's milk** should not be introduced into the diet until **after 1 year of age.** Its protein and mineral content stresses the immature kidney. The young infant cannot fully digest the protein and fat contained in cow's milk.

Meeting Nutritional Needs

The American Academy of Pediatrics recommends that infants receive **breast milk** for the first 6 to 12 months of age. Even a short period of breastfeeding has physiological benefits. If breastfeeding is not possible, the mother should be reassured that commercial formulas can supply the infant with adequate nutrition.

Δ   **Advantages of Breastfeeding**

- Incidence of **otitis media (ear infections)** and **gastrointestinal** and **respiratory disorders** are reduced. This is due to the transfer of antibodies from mother to baby.

- **Carbohydrates, proteins, and fats** in breast milk are predigested for ready absorption.

- Breast milk is **high in omega-3 fatty acids**.

- Breast milk is **low in sodium**.

- **Iron, zinc, and magnesium** in breast milk are highly absorbable.

- **Calcium absorption** is enhanced because the calcium-to-phosphorous ratio is 2:1.

- The risk of **allergies** is reduced.

- Maternal-infant **bonding** is promoted.

Δ   **Breastfeeding Teaching Points**

- The **newborn** is offered the breast immediately after birth and frequently thereafter, nursing for 5 min from each breast.

- The newborn should nurse up to **15 min per breast** by the end of the first week.

- Do not offer the baby any other fluids unless medically indicated.

- The **mother's milk supply** is equal to the demand of the infant.

- Eventually the infant will empty a breast within 5 to 10 min, but may need to continue to suck to meet **comfort needs**.

- Frequent feedings (every 2 hr may be indicated) and manual expression of milk to initiate flow may be needed.

- **Expressed milk** may be refrigerated in sterile bottles for use within 24 hr or may be frozen in sterile containers for up to 3 months.

- **Thaw milk** in the refrigerator. Defrosting or heating in a microwave oven is not recommended because high heat destroys some of the milk's antibodies and may also burn the infant's oral mucosa.

- Do not refreeze thawed milk.

- Avoid consuming freshwater fish or alcohol and limit caffeine.

- Do not take medications unless prescribed by a provider.

Δ **Formula Feeding**

- **Commercial infant formulas provide an alternative** to breast milk. They are modified from cow's milk to provide comparable nutrients.

- An **iron-fortified formula** is recommended by the American Academy of Pediatrics for at least the first 6 months of life or until the infant consumes adequate solid food. After 6 months, formula without added iron may be indicated.

- **Fluoride supplements** may be required if an adequate level is not supplied by the water supply.

- **Wash hands** prior to preparing formula.

- Use **sterile bottles** and **nipples**.

- Precisely follow the **manufacturer's mixing directions**.

- Bottles of mixed formula or open cans of liquid formula require refrigeration. Do not use if the formula has been left at room temperature for 2 hr or longer. Do not reuse partially emptied bottles of formula.

- The formula may be fed chilled, warmed, or at room temperature. Always give formula at approximately the same temperature.

- **Hold the infant** during the feeding with his **head slightly elevated** to facilitate passage of formula into the stomach. **Tilt the bottle** to maintain formula in the nipple and prevent the swallowing of air.

- Do not prop the bottle or put an infant to bed with a bottle. This practice promotes tooth decay.

- The infant should not drink more than 32 oz of formula per 24-hr period unless directed by a provider.

Δ **Weaning**

- Developmentally, the infant is ready for weaning from breast or bottle to a cup **between 5 to 8 months** of age.

- If breastfeeding is eliminated before 5 to 6 months, a bottle should be provided for the infant's **sucking needs**.

- It is best to substitute the cup for one feeding period at a time over a 5- to 7-day period.

- The **nighttime feeding** is often the last to disappear.

- Never allow a child to take a bottle to bed as this promotes dental caries.

- Use this new schedule for a second feeding period and continue at the infant's pace.

- The child may not be ready to wean from the bottle or breast until 12 to 14 months of age.

∆   **Introducing Solid Food**

- Solid food should not be introduced before **4 to 6 months** of age due to the risk of food allergies and stress on the immature kidneys.

- **Indicators for readiness** include: voluntary control of the head and trunk, hunger less than 4 hr after vigorous nursing or intake of 8 oz of formula, and interest of the infant.

- **Iron-fortified rice cereal** should be offered first. **Wheat cereals** should not be introduced until after the first birthday.

- **New foods** should be introduced one at a time over a 5- to 7-day period to observe for **signs of allergy or intolerance**, which may include fussiness, rash, vomiting, diarrhea, or constipation. **Vegetables** are usually added before fruits. **Strained meats** and **egg yolk** may be added between 6 to 8 months.

- Delay the introduction of milk, eggs, wheat, and citrus fruits that may lead to **allergic reactions** in susceptible infants.

- Do not give **peanuts or peanut butter** due to the risk of a severe allergic reaction.

- The infant may be ready for three meals a day with three snacks by 8 months of age.

- **Homemade baby food** is an acceptable feeding option. Do not use canned or packaged foods that are high in sodium. Select fresh or frozen foods. Do not add sugars or other seasonings.

- Open jars of baby food may be stored in the refrigerator for up to 24 hr, provided the baby was not fed directly from the jar.

- By 9 months of age, the infant should be able to eat **table foods** that are **cooked, chopped,** and **unseasoned.**

- Do not feed the infant **honey** because of the risk of **botulism**.

- Appropriate **finger foods** include: ripe banana, toast strips, graham crackers, cheese cubes, noodles, and peeled chunks of apples, pears, or peaches.

Suggested Introduction of Foods

Birth to 4 Months	4 to 6 Months	6 to 9 Months	9 to 12 Months	1 Year
Breast milk or formula	1. Iron-fortified rice cereal 2. Vegetables 3. Fruits	Strained meats and egg yolk	Table foods (cooked, chopped, and unseasoned)	Cow's milk

Nutrition-Related Problems

△ **Colic** is characterized by persistent crying lasting 3 hr or longer per day.

- The cause of colic is unknown, but it usually occurs in the late afternoon, more than 3 days per week for more than 3 weeks. The crying is accompanied by a tense abdomen and legs drawn up to the belly.

- Colic usually resolves by 3 months of age.

- **Breastfeeding mothers** should continue nursing, but **limit caffeine and nicotine intake**.

- If breastfeeding, **eliminating cruciferous vegetables** (cauliflower, broccoli, and Brussels sprouts), cow's milk, onion, and chocolate may be helpful.

- Burping the baby in an upright position or giving some warm water may be helpful.

- Other **comforting techniques** – such as swaddling, carrying the infant, rocking, or repetitive soft sounds – may soothe the infant.

- Most infants grow and gain weight despite colic.

- Reassure the parent that colic is transient and does not indicate more serious problems or a lack of parental ability.

△ **Lactose intolerance** is the inability to digest significant amounts of lactose, the predominant sugar of milk, and is due to inadequate lactase, the enzyme that digests lactose into glucose and galactose.

- Lactose intolerance has an increased prevalence in individuals of Asian, Native American, African, Latino, and Mediterranean descent.

- **Signs and symptoms** include: abdominal distention, flatus, and occasional diarrhea.

- Either **soy-based** (ProSobee® or Isomil®) or **casein hydrolysate** (Nutramigen® or Pregestimil®) **formulas** can be prescribed as alternative formulas for infants who are lactose intolerant.

Δ **Failure to thrive** is inadequate gains in weight and/or height in comparison to established growth and development norms.

- Assess for **signs and symptoms** of congenital defects, central nervous system disorders, or partial intestinal obstruction.

- Assess for **swallowing or sucking problems**.

- Identify **feeding patterns**, especially concerning preparation of formulas.

- Assess for **psychosocial problems**, especially parent-infant bonding.

- Provide **supportive nutritional guidance**. Usually a high-calorie, high-protein diet is indicated.

- Provide supportive parenting guidance.

Δ **Diarrhea** is characterized by the passage of more than three loose, watery stools over a 24-hr period.

- **Overfeeding** and **food intolerances** are common causes of **osmotic diarrhea**.

- **Infectious diarrhea** in the infant is commonly caused by **rotavirus**.

- Mild diarrhea may require no special interventions. Check with the pediatrician for any diet modifications.

- Treatment for moderate diarrhea should begin at home with **oral rehydration solutions**, such as Pedialyte®, Infalyte®, or ReVital® or their generic equivalents. Eight ounces of solution should be given after each loose stool. **Sports drinks are contraindicated**.

- Teach parents **the signs/symptoms of dehydration:** listlessness, sunken eyes, decreased tears, dry mucous membranes, and decreased urine output.

- Breastfed infants should continue nursing.

- Formula-fed infants usually do not require diluted formulas or special formulas.

- **Contact the provider** if signs and symptoms of dehydration are present, or if vomiting, bloody stools, high fever, change in mental status, or refusal to take liquids occurs.

Δ **Constipation** is an inability to evacuate the bowels or difficulty with evacuating the bowels.

- Constipation is not a common problem for breastfed infants.

- It may be caused by **formula** that is too concentrated or by inadequate carbohydrate intake in formula-fed infants.

- Stress the importance of accurate dilution of formula.

- Advise adherence to the recommended amount of formula intake for age.

Nursing Assessments/Data Collection and Interventions

Δ   Nursing assessments should include an **assessment of knowledge base** of the client regarding nutritional guidelines for infants, normal infant growth patterns, breastfeeding, formula feeding, and the progression for the introduction of solid foods.

Δ   Additionally, the **nurse should provide education and references** for the client regarding each of the assessments listed above.

Primary Reference:

Dudek, S. G. (2006). *Nutrition essentials for nursing practice* (5th ed.). Philadelphia: Lippincott Williams & Wilkins.

Additional Resources:

Hockenberry, M. J., Wilson, D., & Winkelstein, M. L. (2005). *Wong's essentials of pediatric nursing* (7th ed.). St. Louis, MO: Mosby.

For more information, visit the American Academy of Pediatrics Web site at: *www.aap.org*.

Chapter 8: Nutrition for Infants

Application Exercises

1. A nurse is preparing to teach an infant nutrition class in a hospital's obstetrics clinic. The nurse has decided to teach expectant mothers about infant feeding problems. Create a list of questions the mothers may ask and develop an outline of appropriate responses.

2. A client who is pregnant tells a nurse that she will be returning to work when her baby is 6 weeks old. She questions if she should attempt to breastfeed for this short period of time. What should the nurse tell her?

3. A mother has brought her 2-month-old infant to the pediatrician's office for a well-baby visit. The infant weighs 15 lb, 2 oz, and her birth weight was 8 lb, 6 oz. The mother states that the baby is drinking approximately 24 oz of formula a day, in addition to eating infant cereal and fruit. She expresses pride that her baby is "fattening up." What teaching should the nurse provide?

4. Identify the order (1-6) in which the following foods should be introduced to an infant with typical development.

   _____ Strained applesauce

   _____ Strained carrots

   _____ Egg yolk

   _____ Iron-fortified rice cereal

   _____ Cow's milk

   _____ Table foods (cooked, chopped, and unseasoned)

5. **True or False:** Mothers who are breastfeeding should use a microwave or boiling water to thaw expressed milk that they previously froze.

6. **True or False:** Soy formulas can serve as an alternative formula for infants with lactose intolerance.

7. **True or False:** Sports drinks can be used for oral rehydration of infants with diarrhea.

8. **True or False:** Infants should be sent to bed with a bottle to fulfill their desire to suck.

9. A new mother has brought her 6-month-old infant in for a routine check-up. The infant's birth weight was 7 lb, 2 oz, head circumference was 35.5 cm (14 in), and length was 48 cm (19 in). The nurse repeats these measurements during the assessment. Which of the following characteristics would pose a concern? (Check all that apply.)

    _____ Head circumference of 41.5 cm (16 in)

    _____ Weight of 13 lb, 0 oz

    _____ Length of 65 cm (25.5 in)

Chapter 8: Nutrition for Infants

Application Exercises Answer Key

1. A nurse is preparing to teach an infant nutrition class in a hospital's obstetrics clinic. The nurse has decided to teach expectant mothers about infant feeding problems. Create a list of questions the mothers may ask and develop an outline of appropriate responses.

What are some of the benefits of breastfeeding?

The incidence of infections is decreased.
Breast milk contains proteins, fats, and carbohydrates that are more easily absorbed by infants.
The risk of developing food allergies is decreased.
Maternal-infant bonding is promoted.

What is colic and is there any way to prevent it?

The cause of colic is unknown, but it usually occurs in the late afternoon hours, more than 3 days per week for more than 3 weeks.
Colic is characterized by crying, a tense abdomen, and the legs drawn up to the belly.
Burping a baby helps to expel swallowed air, thus decreasing gas formation.
Warm water may provide relief.
If breastfeeding, limit caffeine and nicotine and gas-forming foods.
Reassure the mother that babies will grow and gain weight.

If I breastfeed, how will I know that my baby is eating enough?

A baby can empty a breast in 5 min.
During the first 6 to 8 weeks, a baby may nurse every 2 hr.
The more the mother nurses, the more milk is produced.
Weight gain is a key indicator.
A breastfed infant may require iron supplements.

What foods should I feed the baby first?

Feed with formula or breast milk for 4 to 6 months.
Add iron-fortified rice cereal as the first solid food.
Gradually add vegetables, then fruits.
Add strained meats and egg yolk at 6 to 9 months.
Avoid feeding the infant honey and avoid cow's milk until after 1 year of age.

2. A client who is pregnant tells a nurse that she will be returning to work when her baby is 6 weeks old. She questions if she should attempt to breastfeed for this short period of time. What should the nurse tell her?

Instruct the client that breastfeeding for any length of time is beneficial for the infant. During those 6 weeks, the baby receives many antibodies that strengthen the immune system and may also prevent future allergies. Breast milk is the perfect food for the newborn's digestive system, as it contains nutrients that are easily absorbed by the infant's digestive system. You may also ask if she has considered pumping breast milk for the baby to drink while she is away from home.

3. A mother has brought her 2-month-old infant to the pediatrician's office for a well-baby visit. The infant weighs 15 lb, 2 oz, and her birth weight was 8 lb, 6 oz. The mother states that the baby is drinking approximately 24 oz of formula a day, in addition to eating infant cereal and fruit. She expresses pride that her baby is "fattening up." What teaching should the nurse provide?

The introduction of so many foods at this early age increases the risk of developing food allergies. Discuss the expected development and schedule of food introductions with the parent. For example, solid foods should not be introduced until 4 months of age or later.

4. Identify the order (1-6) in which the following foods should be introduced to an infant with typical development.

   __3__ Strained applesauce

   __2__ Strained carrots

   __4__ Egg yolk

   __1__ Iron-fortified rice cereal

   __6__ Cow's milk

   __5__ Table foods (cooked, chopped, and unseasoned)

5. **True or False:** Mothers who are breastfeeding should use a microwave or boiling water to thaw expressed milk that they previously froze.

False: Heating the milk can destroy the antibodies, and it may burn the infant's oral mucosa.

6. **True or False:** Soy formulas can serve as an alternative formula for infants with lactose intolerance.

True

7. **True or False:** Sports drinks can be used for oral rehydration of infants with diarrhea.

False: Sports drinks are not specially formulated for infants. Rather, a specially formulated rehydration drink (Pedialyte®, Infalyte®) should be used.

8. **True or False:** Infants should be sent to bed with a bottle to fulfill their desire to suck.

False: Infants should never be given a bottle when going to bed because it promotes dental caries.

9. A new mother has brought her 6-month-old infant in for a routine check-up. The infant's birth weight was 7 lb, 2 oz, head circumference was 35.5 cm (14 in), and length was 48 cm (19 in). The nurse repeats these measurements during the assessment. Which of the following characteristics would pose a concern? (Check all that apply.)

    __X__ Head circumference of 41.5 cm (16 in)
    __X__ Weight of 13 lb, 0 oz
    _____ Length of 65 cm (25.5 in)

The normal rate of head circumference growth is approximately 1.5 cm (0.6 in) per month. Based on the infant's birth measurements, its head circumference should be around 44.5 cm (17.5 in). Birth weight should at least double by age 6 months. Based on the infant's birth weight, the current weight should be at least 14 lb, 4 oz. The nurse's assessment should begin with an inventory of the infant's eating patterns and sources of nutrition, and then the nurse should provide nutrition counseling as appropriate. Deviations from expected growth patterns may be an indication of an underlying disease process and should be investigated.

Unit 2   Nutrition Across the Lifespan

Chapter 9:   Nutrition for Children
                  Contributor: Kathleen Jones, MEd, RN

↻ NCLEX® Connections:

> **Learning Objective**: Review and apply knowledge within **"Nutrition for Children"** in readiness for performance of the following nutrition nursing activities as outlined by the NCLEX® test plans:
>
> Δ   Recognize and report the client's deviations from growth and development norms.
>
> Δ   Provide nutritional care appropriate to the developmental level of the client.

📖 Key Points

Δ   **Growth rate slows** during the years following infancy.

Δ   Before puberty, children generally grow **2 to 3 inches** in height and gain approximately **5 lb annually**.

Δ   Energy needs and appetite vary with the child's activity level.

Δ   Generally, nutrient needs increase with age.

Δ   **Attitudes** toward food and general food **habits** are established by the age of 5.

Δ   Increasing the variety and texture of foods helps the child develop good food habits.

Δ   Foods like hot dogs, popcorn, peanuts, grapes, raw carrots, celery, peanut butter, tough meat, and candy may cause **choking or aspiration** in the young child.

Δ   Inclusion in **family mealtime** is important for the social development of the young child.

Δ   Group eating becomes a significant means of **socialization** for the school-age child.

Δ **The Food Guide Pyramid for Young Children**, developed by the United States Department of Agriculture (USDA), is the recommended guide for providing adequate nutrition. Children require the same food groups as an adult, but in smaller serving sizes.

Toddlers: 1 to 3 years old

Δ **Nutrition Guidelines**

- Toddlers generally grow 2 to 3 inches in height and gain approximately 5 lb annually.

- **Limit juice** to 4 to 6 oz a day.

- The 1- to 2-year-old child requires **whole cow's milk** to provide adequate fat for the still-growing brain.

- Food serving size is 1 tablespoon for each year of age.

- Exposure to a **new food** may need to occur 8 to 15 times before the child develops an acceptance of it.

- If there is a negative family history for **allergy,** then cow's milk, chocolate, citrus fruits, egg white, seafood, and nut butters may be gradually introduced while monitoring the child for reactions.

- Toddlers prefer **finger foods** because of their increasing autonomy. They also prefer plain foods to mixtures, but usually like macaroni and cheese, spaghetti, and pizza.

- **Regular meal times** and nutritious snacks best meet nutrient needs.

- **Snacks** or **desserts** that are high in sugar, fat, or sodium should be avoided.

- Children are at an increased risk for **choking** until the age of 4.

- Avoid foods that are potential choking hazards (nuts, grapes, hot dogs, peanut butter, raw carrots, tough meats, and popcorn). Always provide adult supervision during snack and meal times. During food preparation, cut small bite-sized pieces to make them easier to swallow and prevent choking. Do not allow the child to engage in drinking or eating during play activities or while lying down.

Δ **Nutritional Concerns/Risks**

- **Iron**

  ◊ **Iron deficiency anemia** is the most common nutritional deficiency disorder in children.

  ◊ **Lean red meats** provide sources of readily absorbable iron.

  ◊ Consuming **vitamin C** (orange juice, tomatoes) with plant sources of iron (beans, raisins, peanut butter, whole grains) will maximize absorption.

◊ Milk should be limited to the recommended quantities (24 oz) because milk is a poor source of iron and may displace the intake of iron-rich foods.

- **Vitamin D**

    ◊ Vitamin D is essential for **bone development**.

    ◊ Recommended vitamin D intake is the same (**5 µg/day**) from birth through age 50. Children require more vitamin D per pound because their bones are growing.

    ◊ **Milk** (cow's and soy) and **fatty fish** are good sources of vitamin D.

    ◊ **Sunlight exposure** leads to vitamin D synthesis. Children who spend large amounts of time inside (watching TV, playing video games) are at an increased risk for vitamin D deficiency.

    ◊ Vitamin D assists in the absorption of calcium into the bones.

Preschoolers: 3 to 5 years

Δ **Nutrition Guidelines**

- Preschoolers generally grow 2 to 3 inches in height and gain approximately 5 lb annually.

- Preschoolers need **13 to 19 g/day of complete protein** in addition to **adequate calcium**, **iron**, **folate,** and **vitamins A** and **C**.

- Preschoolers tend to dislike strong-tasting vegetables, such as cabbage and onions, but like many raw vegetables that are eaten as finger foods.

- **Food jags** (ritualistic preference for one food) are **common and usually short-lived**.

- Food Pyramid guidelines are appropriate, requiring the lowest number of servings per food group.

- Food patterns and preferences are first learned from the family; peers generally start influencing preferences and habits at around age 5.

Δ **Nutritional Concerns/Risks**

- Concerns include **overfeeding**, intake of high-calorie, high-fat, high-sodium **snacks, soft drinks, and juices,** and **inadequate intake of fruits and vegetables**.

    ◊ Be alert to the appropriate serving size of foods (1 tablespoon per year of age).

    ◊ Avoid high-fat and high-sugar snacks.

    ◊ Provide daily physical activities that encourage running, climbing, jumping, etc.

    ◊ May switch to skim or 1% low-fat milk after age 2.

- **Iron deficiency anemia** (see previous information for Toddlers).

- **Lead poisoning** is a risk for children under age 6 because children frequently place objects in their mouths that may contain lead and they have a higher rate of intestinal absorption.

  ◊ Feed children at frequent intervals, since more lead is absorbed on an empty stomach.

  ◊ Inadequate intake of calories, calcium, iron, zinc, and phosphorous may increase susceptibility.

School-Age Children: 6 to 12 years

Δ **Nutrition Guidelines**

- School-age children generally grow 2 to 3 inches in height and gain approximately 5 lb annually.

- Diet should provide **variety**, **balance**, and **moderation**, following the Food Pyramid recommendations.

- Young athletes need to meet energy, protein, and fluid needs.

- Teach children to make healthy food selections.

- Children enjoy learning how to safely prepare nutritious snacks.

- Children need to learn to eat snacks only when hungry, not when bored or inactive.

Δ **Nutrition Concerns/Risks**

- **Skipping breakfast** occurs in about **10% of children**.

  ◊ Optimum performance in school is dependent on a nutritious breakfast.

  ◊ Children who regularly eat breakfast tend to have an age-appropriate body mass index.

- **Overweight/obesity** affects at least 20% of children.

  ◊ Greater psychosocial implications exist for children than adults.

  ◊ Overweight children tend to be obese as adults.

  ◊ **Prevention** is the key: Encourage healthy eating habits, decrease fats and sugars (empty-calorie foods), and increase the level of physical activity.

  ◊ A **weight-loss program** directed by a primary care provider is indicated for children who are more than **40% overweight**.

  ◊ Praise the child's abilities and skills.

  ◊ Never use food as a reward or punishment.

Nursing Assessments/Data Collection and Interventions

Δ   Nursing assessments should include the parent or caretaker's knowledge base of the child's nutritional requirements and nutritional concerns with regard to age. The nurse should also provide education for the parent/caretaker and the child, when appropriate, about nutritional recommendations.

Primary Reference:

Dudek, S. G. (2006). *Nutrition essentials for nursing practice* (5th ed.). Philadelphia: Lippincott Williams & Wilkins.

Additional Resources:

For more information, visit the American Academy of Pediatrics Web site at: *www.aap.org*.

For more information on the Food Guide Pyramid, visit the USDA's MyPyramid.gov at: *www.MyPyramid.gov*.

Chapter 9: Nutrition for Children

Application Exercises

1. Listed below is a typical lunch for a school-age child. Complete the chart to demonstrate how to make over this child's lunch to include healthy and nutrient-rich foods.

Typical Lunch	Lunch Makeover
Bologna and American cheese sandwich (white bread)	
Potato chips	
Canned sliced peaches	
Brownie	
Fruit-flavored drink	

2. Indicate – with a yes or no – which of the following snack foods are appropriate for toddlers. For those snacks that are not appropriate, explain why.

_____ Raw carrot sticks

_____ Graham crackers

_____ Marshmallows

_____ Apple slices

_____ Raisins

_____ Popcorn

_____ Yogurt

_____ Jelly beans

_____ Cheese cubes

_____ Grapes cut into small pieces

3. A mother brings her 3-year-old son in for a routine appointment. She states that she is concerned that her son wants to eat macaroni and cheese for every meal. What information is important to share with the mother?

4. Select the activities that are important in preventing unhealthy weight gain in children.

_____ Eliminate complex carbohydrates.

_____ Drink 2% or skim milk.

_____ Decrease saturated fats in the diet.

_____ Use food as a reward when the child meets expectations.

_____ Provide nutrient-dense snack foods.

_____ Limit video games and television viewing.

_____ Promote 1 hr of intense physical activity after school and several hours during the weekend.

_____ Plan family hikes, skating, and swimming.

_____ Compare child to peers.

_____ Serve milk and cookies after school.

5. Explain why adequate vitamin D intake is important for children. Name two sources of vitamin D.

6. List five examples of iron-rich foods.

7. **True or False:** Milk consumption should be encouraged because it is a great source of iron.

8. **True or False:** Consuming sources of vitamin D with plant sources of iron will increase iron absorption.

9. **True or False:** Iron deficiency anemia is the most common nutrient deficiency in children.

10. A nurse has just finished collecting the height and weight of a 4-year-old boy. His mother states that she is concerned with his weight gain over the last year. The boy has gained 11 lb and has grown nearly 7 inches over the last 24 months. What information is important to share with this mother?

Chapter 9: Nutrition for Children

Application Exercises Answer Key

1. Listed below is a typical lunch for a school-age child. Complete the chart to demonstrate how to make over this child's lunch to include healthy and nutrient-rich foods.

Typical Lunch	Lunch Makeover
Bologna and American cheese sandwich (white bread)	**Low-fat, high-quality protein; fiber (Turkey on whole wheat, mozzarella cheese sticks)**
Potato chips	**Crunchy texture; source of vitamins and minerals (Carrot sticks, celery with light ranch dressing or pretzels)**
Canned sliced peaches	**Fresh fruit to increase fiber (Apple)**
Brownie	**Low-fat, low-sugar; minerals (Fat-free animal cookies or yogurt)**
Fruit-flavored drink	**Drink to provide vitamins, calcium; fat-free or low-fat, no sucrose (Skim milk or 2% milk)**

2. Indicate – with a yes or no – which of the following snack foods are appropriate for toddlers. For those snacks that are not appropriate, explain why.

  _No_ Raw carrot sticks – **Pose a choking hazard**

  Yes Graham crackers

  _No_ Marshmallows – **Difficult to chew/swallow; high-sugar, empty-calorie snack**

  Yes Apple slices

  _No_ Raisins – **Difficult to chew; choking hazard**

  _No_ Popcorn – **Kernel shells pose a choking hazard**

  Yes Yogurt

  _No_ Jelly beans – **Difficult to chew/swallow; high-sugar, empty-calorie snack**

  Yes Cheese cubes

  Yes Grapes cut into small pieces

3. A mother brings her 3-year-old son in for a routine appointment. She states that she is concerned that her son wants to eat macaroni and cheese for every meal. What information is important to share with the mother?

The nurse should explain that the child is experiencing what is referred to as a food jag, a ritualistic preference for one food. The nurse should reassure the mother that this is a normal stage of development for a child of this age and that food jags usually disappear in time.

4. Select the activities that are important in preventing unhealthy weight gain in children.

_____ Eliminate complex carbohydrates.

__x__ Drink 2% or skim milk.

__x__ Decrease saturated fats in the diet.

_____ Use food as a reward when the child meets expectations.

__x__ Provide nutrient-dense snack foods.

__x__ Limit video games and television viewing.

__x__ Promote 1 hr of intense physical activity after school and several hours during the weekend.

__x__ Plan family hikes, skating, and swimming.

_____ Compare child to peers.

_____ Serve milk and cookies after school.

5. Explain why adequate vitamin D intake is important for children. Name two sources of vitamin D.

Vitamin D is essential for the development of healthy bones. It is especially important in children because their bones are newly formed and continually growing. Vitamin D also aids in the absorption of calcium into the bones. Sunlight exposure, milk (both cow's and soy), and fatty fish are all sources of vitamin D.

6. List five examples of iron-rich foods.

Iron-rich foods include lean red meats, beans, raisins, peanut butter, and whole grains.

7. **True or False:** Milk consumption should be encouraged because it is a great source of iron.

False: Milk consumption should be limited to the age-appropriate recommended amount because it is a poor source of iron and it may replace other iron-rich foods.

8. **True or False:** Consuming sources of vitamin D with plant sources of iron will increase iron absorption.

False: Vitamin C increases the absorption of iron.

9. **True or False:** Iron deficiency anemia is the most common nutrient deficiency in children.

True

10. A nurse has just finished collecting the height and weight of a 4-year-old boy. His mother states that she is concerned with his weight gain over the last year. The boy has gained 11 lb and has grown nearly 7 inches over the last 24 months. What information is important to share with this mother?

It is important to share with the mother that her son is demonstrating appropriate growth in both height and weight. The nurse should also inform the mother that children should gain approximately 5 lb and grow 2 to 3 inches annually until they reach puberty. Also, encourage the mother to provide wholesome, nutrient-dense foods and activities that promote physical exercise. Lastly, instruct her to continue with regular physicals for her son.

Unit 2   Nutrition Across the Lifespan

Chapter 10:   Nutrition for Adolescents
                         Contributor: Kathleen Jones, MEd, RN

↻ NCLEX® Connections:

> **Learning Objective**: Review and apply knowledge within "**Nutrition for Adolescents**" in readiness for performance of the following nutrition nursing activities as outlined by the NCLEX® test plans:
>
> Δ   Recognize and report the client's deviations from growth and development norms.
>
> Δ   Provide nutritional care appropriate to the developmental level of the client.

📖 Key Points

Δ   The rate of growth during adolescence is second only to the rate in infancy, and **nutritional needs for energy, protein, calcium, iron, and zinc increase** at the onset of puberty and the growth spurt.

Δ   Approximately 15 to 20% of adult height and 50% of adult weight are gained during adolescence.

Δ   **Girls' growth spurt** usually begins at age 10 or 11, peaks at 12 years, and is completed by age 17. Girls' energy requirements are less than that of boys, because they experience less growth of muscle and bone tissue and more fat deposition.

Δ   **Boys' growth spurt** begins at age 12 or 13, peaks at 14 years, and is completed by age 21.

Δ   **Eating habits** of adolescents are often inadequate in meeting recommended nutritional intake goals.

Nutritional Considerations

Δ   **Energy requirements** average 2,000 cal/day for a 15-year-old girl and 4,000 cal/day for a 15-year-old boy.

Δ   The United State Department of Agriculture (USDA) reports that **the average U.S. adolescent** consumes a diet deficient in folate, vitamins A and E, iron, zinc, magnesium, calcium, and fiber. This trend is more pronounced in females than males.

Δ   Diets of adolescents generally exceed current recommendations for total fat, saturated fat, cholesterol, sodium, and sugar.

Nutritional Risks

Δ   **Eating and snacking patterns** promote essential nutrient deficiencies (calcium, vitamins, iron, fiber) and overconsumption of sugars, fat, and sodium.

- Adolescents tend to **skip meals**, especially breakfast, and eat more meals away from home.

- Foods are often selected from **vending machines**, **convenience stores**, and **fast food** restaurants; these foods are usually high in fat, sugar, and sodium.

- **Carbonated beverages** may replace milk and fruit juices in the diet with resulting deficiencies in vitamin C, riboflavin, phosphorous, and calcium.

Δ   Adolescents have **increased need for iron**.

- Girls age 14 to 18 require 15 mg of iron to support expansion of blood volume and blood loss during menstruation.

- Boys age 14 to 18 require 11 mg of iron to support expansion of muscle mass and blood volume.

Δ   **Inadequate calcium intake** may predispose the adolescent to osteoporosis later in life, since optimal bone density may not be achieved.

- Forty-five percent of bone mass is added during adolescence.

- If calcium intake is low, the body maintains normal blood-calcium levels by drawing calcium from the bones.

- Adolescents require **at least 1,300 mg of calcium a day**, which may be achieved by 3 to 4 servings from the dairy food group.

Δ   **Dieting**

- **Social pressure** to be thin and the stigma of obesity can lead to unhealthy eating practices and poor body image, especially in females.

- Boys are more susceptible to using **supplements** and **high-protein drinks** in order to build muscle mass and improve athletic performance. Some athletes do restrict calories to maintain or achieve a lower weight.

- **Eating disorders** may follow self-imposed crash diets for weight loss.

Δ   **Anorexia Nervosa**

- Females are primarily affected at 12 to 13 years and 19 to 20 years.

- Anorexia nervosa is a condition of **self-imposed starvation**.

- Affected females usually are **high-achievers** who may suffer **poor self-esteem, feel unloved,** are **passive**, and have a **distorted image** of their own bodies and "thinness."

- **Physical findings** include amenorrhea (absence of menses), brittle hair, dry skin, and hypotension (low blood pressure).

- **Long-term health risks** of anorexia nervosa include permanent brain damage, sterility, multi-organ damage, and heart failure. Of chronically affected individuals, one in five to seven die from complications.

Δ   **Bulimia Nervosa**

- Bulimia nervosa is characterized by **repeated episodes of binge eating** (up to 11,500 calories of high-fat, high-sugar foods), **followed by recurrent purging** through laxatives, self-induced vomiting, emetics, diuretics, or compulsive exercise.

- Episodes may be triggered by stressful events.

- The condition may go undiagnosed because the **eating behavior is secretive**.

- Bulimia nervosa is more frequent than anorexia, probably affecting up to 20% of female college students.

- **Physical findings** include weight fluctuations, calloused index finger from self-induced emesis, poor dental health, fatigue, sore throat, dehydration, acid-base imbalances, and cardiac arrhythmias.

- **Long-term health risks** of bulimia include esophagitis (inflammation of the esophagus), oral mucosal irritation, and irreversible tooth enamel erosion.

Δ   **Adolescent Pregnancy**

- The physiologic demands of a growing fetus compromise the adolescent's needs for her own unfinished growth and development.

- Inconsistent eating and poor food choices place the adolescent at risk for anemia, pregnancy-induced hypertension, gestational diabetes, premature labor, spontaneous abortion, and delivery of a low-birth-weight infant.

Nursing Assessments/Data Collection and Interventions

△ Nursing assessments should include a determination of the adolescent's:

- Typical 24-hr food intake.

- Weight patterns, current weight, and ideal body weight.

- Attitude about current weight.

- Use of nutritional supplements, vitamins, and minerals.

- Medical history and use of prescription medications.

- Use of over-the-counter medications, street drugs, alcohol, and tobacco.

- Level of daily physical activity.

△ The nurse should also assess for **signs** and **symptoms** of an **eating disorder**. This may include an evaluation of the adolescent's laboratory values.

△ Nursing assessments should also include **health promoting strategies** for the adolescent.

- Educate the adolescent on the use of the **Food Pyramid** to meet energy and nutrient needs with three regular meals and snacks.

- Stress the importance of meeting **calcium needs** by including low-fat milk, yogurt, and cheese in the diet.

- Educate the adolescent on how to select/prepare **nutrient-dense snack foods:** unbuttered, unsalted popcorn, pretzels, fresh fruit, string cheese, smoothies made with low-fat yogurt, skim milk, or reduced-calorie fruit juice and fresh fruit, and raw vegetables with low-fat dips.

- Encourage participation in **vigorous physical activity** at least three times a week.

- Refer pregnant adolescents to the Women, Infant, and Children (WIC) nutrition subsidy program.

- Provide individual and group counseling for teens with signs and symptoms of eating disorders.

Primary Reference:

Dudek, S. G. (2006). *Nutrition essentials for nursing practice* (5th ed.). Philadelphia: Lippincott Williams & Wilkins.

Chapter 10: Nutrition for Adolescents

Application Exercises

1. Which of the following foods selected by a teen indicates an understanding of healthy snacks? (Check all that apply.)

　　　_____ Fried onion rings

　　　_____ Carrot sticks with low-fat ranch dip

　　　_____ Cheese and crackers

　　　_____ Unbuttered popcorn

　　　_____ Chocolate cake and whole milk

　　　_____ Chips and dip

　　　_____ Low-fat milk shake

　　　_____ Frozen low-fat yogurt

　　　_____ Hot dog

　　　_____ Brownie sundae

　　　_____ Low-fat cheese pizza

　　　_____ Donut and coffee

2. An adolescent girl arrives for a routine physical. Her mother states that she has reported fatigue for the last 6 weeks and that she is having difficulty staying awake during school hours. What is one possible explanation for the adolescent's extreme fatigue? Include rationale.

3. An adolescent girl is 14 weeks pregnant. She is attending her first prenatal care appointment. What information is important to share with her regarding her nutritional requirements?

4. **True or False:** Anorexia nervosa is an eating disorder characterized by periods of binge eating followed by purging.

5. **True or False:** Bulimia nervosa may go undiagnosed because the unhealthy behavior often occurs in seclusion.

6. **True or False:** Social pressure to be thin and the stigma of obesity are factors in developing distorted body images and eating disorders.

7. **True or False:** Boys are unaffected by eating disorders.

8. Why is achieving adequate calcium intake important?

9. During a routine physical, a mother states that she is concerned that her 11-year-old daughter has surpassed her 11-year-old twin brother in height and weight. The mother asks if she should reduce her daughter's caloric intake to keep her from gaining too much weight. What information is important to share with the mother?

Chapter 10: Nutrition for Adolescents

Application Exercises Answer Key

1. Which of the following foods selected by a teen indicates an understanding of healthy snacks? (Check all that apply.)

    _____ Fried onion rings

    _x_ Carrot sticks with low-fat ranch dip

    _x_ Cheese and crackers

    _x_ Unbuttered popcorn

    _____ Chocolate cake and whole milk

    _____ Chips and dip

    _x_ Low-fat milk shake

    _x_ Frozen low-fat yogurt

    _____ Hot dog

    _____ Brownie sundae

    _x_ Low-fat cheese pizza

    _____ Donut and coffee

2. An adolescent girl arrives for a routine physical. Her mother states that she has reported fatigue for the last 6 weeks and that she is having difficulty staying awake during school hours. What is one possible explanation for the adolescent's extreme fatigue? Include rationale.

The girl may be experiencing iron deficiency anemia. The nurse should explain that adolescent girls have an increased need for iron, and deficiency can result from the growth spurt and blood loss from menses.

3. An adolescent girl is 14 weeks pregnant. She is attending her first prenatal care appointment. What information is important to share with her regarding her nutritional requirements?

The nurse should explain to her that a growing fetus places great physiologic demands on the mother that can compromise her own needs for her unfinished growth and development. The nurse should also share that poor food choices of nutrient-poor foods and inconsistent eating patterns can place her at risk for developing anemia, pregnancy-induced hypertension, gestational diabetes, premature labor, spontaneous abortion, and delivery of a low-birth-weight infant.

4. **True or False:** Anorexia nervosa is an eating disorder characterized by periods of binge eating followed by purging.

False: Anorexia nervosa is characterized by self-imposed starvation. Bulimia nervosa is characterized by binge eating and subsequent purging.

5. **True or False:** Bulimia nervosa may go undiagnosed because the unhealthy behavior often occurs in seclusion.

True

6. **True or False:** Social pressure to be thin and the stigma of obesity are factors in developing distorted body images and eating disorders.

True

7. **True or False:** Boys are unaffected by eating disorders.

False: Although girls are more commonly affected by eating disorders, boys are still affected.

8. Why is achieving adequate calcium intake important?

Forty-five percent of bone mass is achieved during the adolescent years. Failure to achieve adequate calcium intake leads to the withdrawal of calcium from the bones to maintain adequate blood-calcium levels. This leads to an increased risk of developing osteoporosis later in life.

9. During a routine physical, a mother states that she is concerned that her 11-year-old daughter has surpassed her 11-year-old twin brother in height and weight. The mother asks if she should reduce her daughter's caloric intake to keep her from gaining too much weight. What information is important to share with the mother?

The nurse should inform the mother that her daughter's growth is within the expected range. Tell her that girls' growth spurts usually begin at age 10 or 11, peak at 12 years, and are likely completed by 17 years of age. Also share with her that boys' growth spurts usually begin later at age 12 or 13, peak at 14, and are usually not completed until age 21. Lastly, encourage the mother to provide nutrient-dense foods to support the rapid growth that is experienced during adolescence.

Unit 2   Nutrition Across the Lifespan

Chapter 11:   Nutrition for Adults and Older Adults
Contributor: Lynne B. Welch, EdD, APRN, BC-FNP

NCLEX® Connections:

Learning Objective: Review and apply knowledge within "**Nutrition for Adults and Older Adults**" in readiness for performance of the following nutrition nursing activities as outlined by the NCLEX® test plans:

Δ   Recognize and report the client's deviations from growth and development norms.

Δ   Provide nutritional care appropriate to the developmental level of the client.

Key Points

Δ   Nurses should assess the **nutritional, physical,** and **mental health** of adults and older adults.

Δ   A **balanced diet** for all adults consists of **40 to 55% carbohydrate** and **10 to 20% fat** (with no more than 30% fat).

Δ   The recommended amount for **protein** is unchanged in adults and older adults; however, many nutrition experts believe that protein requirements increase somewhat in older adults.

Δ   **Older adults** need to **reduce total caloric intake** due to the decrease in basal metabolic rate that occurs in response to the decrease in lean body mass that occurs with aging.

Δ   Reduced caloric intake predisposes the older adult for development of nutrient deficiencies.

Δ   **Regular exercise** is encouraged for all adults.

Δ   **Older adults** may have **physical, mental,** and **social changes** that affect their ability to purchase, prepare, and digest foods and nutrients.

Δ   **Dehydration** is the most common fluid and electrolyte imbalance in older adults. Fluid needs increase with medication-induced fluid losses. Some disease processes necessitate fluid restrictions.

Nutritional Concerns

△ A **24-hr dietary intake** is helpful in determining the need for dietary education.

△ **Older adults** may have **oral problems** such as ill-fitting dentures and difficulty chewing or swallowing. Older adults may have decreased salivation or poor dental health.

△ **Older adults** have **decreased cellular function and reduced body reserves**, leading to decreased absorption of B_{12}, folic acid vitamins, and calcium, as well as reductions in insulin production and sensitivity.

△ Decreased elasticity of blood vessels can lead to **hypertension**.

△ Kidneys (renal) regulate the amount of potassium and sodium in the blood stream. **Renal function** can decrease as much as 50% in older adults.

△ Older adults have decreased lean muscle mass. **Exercise** can help to counteract muscle mass loss.

△ Loss of calcium can result in **decreased bone density** in older adults.

△ Cell-mediated immunity decreases as an individual ages.

Balanced Diet and Nutrient Needs

△ **MyPyramid**, developed by the United States Department of Agriculture (USDA), suggests the following **daily food intake** for adults and older adults who get less than 30 min of moderate physical activity most days:

	Men			Women		
	19-30	31-50	51+	19-30	31-50	51+
Calories	2,400	2,200	2,000	2,000	1,800	1,600
Fruits	2 cups	2 cups	2 cups	2 cups	1 ½ cups	1 ½ cups
Vegetables	3 cups	3 cups	2 ½ cups	2 ½ cups	2 ½ cups	2 cups
Grains	8 oz	7 oz	6 oz	6 oz	6 oz	5 oz
Meats and Beans	6 ½ oz	6 oz	5 ½ oz	5 ½ oz	5 oz	5 oz
Milk	3 cups	3 cups	3 cups	3 cups	3 cups	3 cups
Oils	7 tsp	6 tsp	6 tsp	6 tsp	5 tsp	5 tsp

Source: United States Department of Agriculture. *MyPyramid.gov*. Retrieved May 4, 2006, from http://www. mypyramid.gov/global_nav/media_mypyramid_patterns.html

△ **Grain group**: Select whole grains.

△ **Vegetables**: Select more **orange** and **dark green leafy vegetables**.

Δ **Fruits**: May select fresh, dried, canned, or juices. **Avoid** those with **added sugar**.

Δ **Milk, yogurt, and cheese group**: One cup of milk or plain yogurt is equivalent to 1 ½ oz natural cheese or 2 oz processed cheese.

Δ **Meat and bean group**: Includes meat, fish, poultry, dry beans, eggs, and nuts. One ounce equals: 1 oz meat, fish, or poultry (baked, grilled, or broiled); ¼ cup cooked dry beans; 1 egg; 1 Tbsp peanut butter; or ½ oz nuts. **Use lean meats**.

Δ **Oils**: **Use vegetable oils** (**except palm and coconut**). 1 Tbsp of oil equals 3 tsp equivalent; 1 Tbsp mayonnaise equals 2 ½ tsp dietary intake; and 1 oz nuts equals 3 tsp oils (except hazelnut, which equals 4 tsp).

Δ **Discretionary calories**: From 132 to 362 discretionary calories are permitted per day. These add up quickly and can be from more than one food group.

Δ **Minerals**: Calcium requirements increase for older adults because the efficiency of calcium absorption decreases with age.

Δ **Vitamins**: Vitamins A, D, C, E, B_6, and B_{12} may be decreased in older adults. Supplemental vitamins are recommended.

Regular Exercise

Δ All adults should exercise at a moderate or vigorous pace for at least **30 min per day** for **3 to 7 days a week**.

Δ Physical activity must **increase heart rate** to be relevant. Moderate activities include gardening/yard work, golf, dancing, and walking briskly.

Δ The **loss of lean muscle** mass that is part of normal aging **can be decreased** with regular exercise. The loss of lean muscle may be associated with a decrease in total protein and insulin sensitivity.

Δ Regular exercise can also **improve bone density, relieve depression**, and **enhance cardiovascular** and **respiratory function**.

Potential Impact of Physical, Mental, and Social Changes

Δ **Diseases and their treatments** may interfere with nutrient and food absorption and utilization.

• Aging adults are at an increased risk for developing **osteoporosis** (decreasing total bone mass and deterioration of bone tissue). Adequate calcium and vitamin D intake along with regular weight-bearing exercise are important for maximizing bone density.

• **Osteoarthritis (OA)** causes significant disability and pain in the older adult client. OA can limit mobility and present difficulty in obtaining and preparing proper foods.

- **Alzheimer's disease** is a form of dementia commonly seen in clients age 65 and older. This form of dementia causes impairments in memory and judgment, making shopping, storing, and cooking food difficult.

Δ Certain **medications** (diuretics for example) **for hypertension** can cause sodium or potassium losses.

Δ **Arthritis** can interfere with the purchase or preparation of foods.

Δ **Loss of smell and vision** interfere with the interest in eating food.

Δ **Body mass index (BMI)** should be **between 18.5 and 24.9**. There is increased risk for both overweight and underweight older adults. Overweight adults are more prone to hypertension, diabetes, and cardiovascular events.

Δ Older adults may have **difficulty chewing,** in which case mincing or chopping food is helpful. They may also have difficulty swallowing food, in which case thickened liquids may decrease the risk for aspiration.

Δ Social isolation, loss of a spouse, and mental deterioration may all cause poor nutrition in the adult and older adult population. **Encourage socialization** and refer to a senior center or program.

Δ A fixed income may make it difficult for older adults to purchase needed foods. Refer to **food programs, senior centers,** and **food banks.** Meals on Wheels is available for housebound older adults.

Fluid Intake

Δ The long-held standard of consuming **eight glasses (8 oz)** of liquid per day has been tempered by evidence that dehydration is not imminent even when less than 64 oz of fluid was consumed.

Δ **Solid foods** provide varying amounts of water, making it possible to get adequate fluid despite low beverage intake.

Δ For healthy adults, it is generally acceptable to allow **normal drinking and eating habits** to **provide needed fluids**.

Δ Encourage **water** and **natural juices**; discourage drinking only soda pop and other liquids that have caffeine.

Nursing Assessments/Data Collection and Interventions

Δ Nursing assessments should include a **dietary profile** of the adult or older adult. Medical history, medication regimen, mobility, social practices, mental status, and financial circumstances are important components of the assessment. The nurse should provide **education** about proper dietary practices for the adult and older adult while additionally providing **referrals** to community agencies when appropriate.

Primary Reference:

Dudek, S. G. (2006). *Nutrition essentials for nursing practice* (5th ed.). Philadelphia: Lippincott Williams & Wilkins.

Additional Resources:

Grosvenor, M. B., & Smolin, L. A. (2002). *Nutrition: From science to life*. Indianapolis, IN: Wiley.

Mahan, L. K., & Escott-Stump, S. (1996). *Krause's food, nutrition and diet therapy* (10th ed.). Philadelphia: W.B. Saunders Company.

Stanfield, P. S., & Hui, Y. H. (2003). *Nutrition and diet therapy: Self-instructional modules* (4th ed.). Sudbury, MA: Jones and Bartlett Publishers.

For more information on the Food Pyramid, visit the USDA's MyPyramid.gov at: *www.MyPyramid.gov*.

Chapter 11: Nutrition for Adults and Older Adults

Application Exercises

1. A 54-year-old female client is newly diagnosed with hypertension. She is taking two new diuretics for her condition. What information is important to share with her regarding side effects and potential nutrition complications?

2. **True or False:** Older adults should refrain from exercising due to their decreased flexibility.

3. **True or False:** Adequate fluid intake can be achieved by healthy older adults from their regular eating and drinking habits.

4. **True or False:** Calcium intake is not as important for adults because their bones are done growing.

5. **True or False:** Social isolation can contribute to poor nutrition.

6. Which of the following factors predispose an older adult to nutrient deficiencies? (Check all that apply.)

    _____ Well-fitting dentures

    _____ Recommended decrease in total caloric intake

    _____ Loss of a spouse

    _____ Extensive medication regimen

    _____ Decreased mobility

    _____ Living on a fixed income

    _____ Participating in an exercise program at a local senior center

7. A nurse is providing discharge instructions to a 71-year-old male client who suffered a broken leg 3 weeks earlier. When reviewing his nutritional recommendations, he states that he doesn't like to take calcium supplements because they are large and difficult for him to swallow. What information is important to share with him?

Chapter 11: Nutrition for Adults and Older Adults

Application Exercises Answer Key

1. A 54-year-old female client is newly diagnosed with hypertension. She is taking two new diuretics for her condition. What information is important to share with her regarding side effects and potential nutrition complications?

The nurse should explain that hypertension is a common ailment of aging adults that can be a result of the decrease in the elasticity of blood vessels. Additionally, renal function can decrease up to 50%. The nurse should inform the client that her medications can predispose her to sodium and potassium losses.

2. **True or False:** Older adults should refrain from exercising due to their decreased flexibility.

False: Exercise is encouraged for all adults. It can reduce the amount of lean muscle mass that is lost due to the aging process, and it can also improve bone density, relieve depression, and improve cardiovascular and respiratory function.

3. **True or False:** Adequate fluid intake can be achieved by healthy older adults from their regular eating and drinking habits.

True

4. **True or False:** Calcium intake is not as important for adults because their bones are done growing.

False: Calcium intake should be increased for adults to prevent calcium being used from bone stores to maintain adequate blood levels.

5. **True or False:** Social isolation can contribute to poor nutrition.

True

6. Which of the following factors predispose an older adult to nutrient deficiencies? (Check all that apply.)

       _____ Well-fitting dentures

       __x__ Recommended decrease in total caloric intake

       __x__ Loss of a spouse

       __x__ Extensive medication regimen

       __x__ Decreased mobility

       __x__ Living on a fixed income

       _____ Participating in an exercise program at a local senior center

7. A nurse is providing discharge instructions to a 71-year-old male client who suffered a broken leg 3 weeks earlier. When reviewing his nutritional recommendations, he states that he doesn't like to take calcium supplements because they are large and difficult for him to swallow. What information is important to share with him?

The nurse should first explain the importance of calcium in maintaining his current bone density. Although bone formation is completed in young adulthood, it is important to continue to achieve adequate oral intake to ensure that bone density is not compromised to maintain blood calcium levels. The nurse should encourage the client to obtain his calcium from foods if he is unable to swallow the pill. Examples of foods high in calcium are low-fat milk, cheeses, and yogurt. The client could also buy juices fortified with calcium. Lastly, the nurse should encourage the client to begin weight-bearing exercise when appropriate.

Unit 3   Clinical Nutrition and Therapeutic Diets

Chapter 12:   Hospital Diets
                 Contributor: Jackie H. Jones, EdD, RN

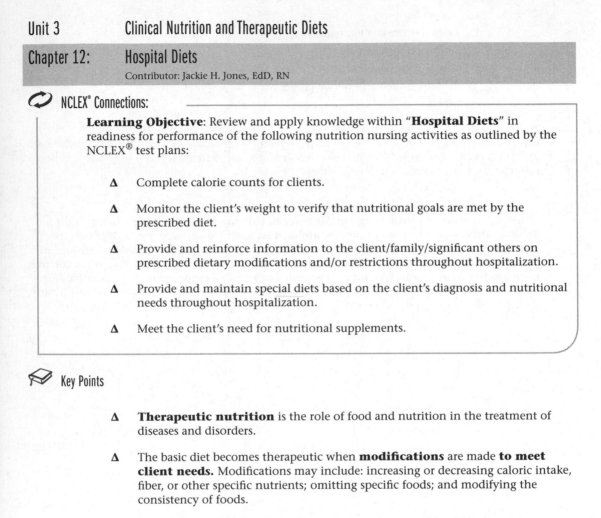

NCLEX® Connections:

> **Learning Objective**: Review and apply knowledge within "**Hospital Diets**" in readiness for performance of the following nutrition nursing activities as outlined by the NCLEX® test plans:
>
> Δ   Complete calorie counts for clients.
>
> Δ   Monitor the client's weight to verify that nutritional goals are met by the prescribed diet.
>
> Δ   Provide and reinforce information to the client/family/significant others on prescribed dietary modifications and/or restrictions throughout hospitalization.
>
> Δ   Provide and maintain special diets based on the client's diagnosis and nutritional needs throughout hospitalization.
>
> Δ   Meet the client's need for nutritional supplements.

Key Points

Δ   **Therapeutic nutrition** is the role of food and nutrition in the treatment of diseases and disorders.

Δ   The basic diet becomes therapeutic when **modifications** are made **to meet client needs.** Modifications may include: increasing or decreasing caloric intake, fiber, or other specific nutrients; omitting specific foods; and modifying the consistency of foods.

Δ   When the gastrointestinal tract is used to provide nourishment, it is referred to as **enteral nutrition**. Whenever possible, regular oral feedings are preferred.

Δ   Nurses should collaborate with the dietician for nutritional or dietary concerns.

Types of Therapeutic Diets

Δ **Clear Liquid Diet**

- Consists of foods that are clear and liquid at room temperature.

- It primarily consists of **water** and **carbohydrates**. The clear liquid diet requires minimal digestion, leaves minimal residue, and is non-gas forming. It is nutritionally inadequate and should not be used long term.

- **Indications** for a clear liquid diet include acute illness, reduction of colon fecal material prior to certain diagnostic tests and procedures, acute gastrointestinal disorders, and, in some instances, postoperative recovery.

- **Acceptable foods** are water, tea, coffee, fat-free broth, carbonated beverages, clear juices, ginger ale, and gelatin.

- Caffeine consumption should be limited as it can lead to increased hydrochloric acid and stomach upset.

Δ **Full Liquid Diet**

- Consists of foods that are liquid at room temperature.

- Full liquid diets offer **more variety and nutritional support** than a **clear liquid** diet and can supply adequate amounts of energy and nutrients.

- **Acceptable foods** include: all liquids on a clear liquid diet, all forms of milk, soups, strained fruits and vegetables, vegetable and fruit juices, eggnog, plain ice cream and sherbet, refined or strained cereals, and puddings.

- If used more than 2 to 3 days, high-protein, high-calorie supplements should be considered.

- **Indications** include a transition from liquid to soft diets, postoperative recovery, acute gastritis, febrile conditions, and/or intolerance of solid foods.

- This diet provides oral nourishment for clients having difficulty chewing or swallowing solid foods; however, clients with dysphagia (difficulty swallowing) should be cautious with liquids unless they are thickened appropriately.

- This diet is **contraindicated** for clients who have **lactose intolerance** or **hypercholesterolemia**. Lactose-reduced milk and dairy products should be used when possible.

Δ **Blenderized Liquid (Pureed) Diet**

- Consists of liquids and foods that have been pureed to liquid form.

- The **composition** and **consistency** of a pureed diet **varies**, depending on the client's needs.

- Pureed diets can be modified with regard to calories, protein, fat, or other nutrients based on the dietary needs of the client.

- Adding broth, milk, gravy, cream, soup, tomato sauce, or fruit juice to foods in place of water provides additional calories and nutritional value.

- Each food is pureed separately to preserve individual flavor.

- **Indications** for use include clients with chewing or swallowing difficulties, oral or facial surgery, or wired jaws.

Δ **Soft (Bland, Low-Fiber) Diet**

- A soft diet contains **whole foods** that are **low in fiber, lightly seasoned, and easily digested**.

- Food supplements or between-meal snacks are used to add calories.

- Food textures may be smooth, creamy, or crisp. Fruits, vegetables, coarse breads and cereals, beans, and other potentially gas-forming foods are excluded.

- **Indications** for this diet include clients transitioning between full liquid and regular diets, or those with acute infections, chewing difficulties, or gastrointestinal disorders.

Δ **Mechanical Soft Diet**

- A mechanical soft diet is a **regular diet** that has been **modified in texture**. The diet composition may be altered for specific nutrient needs.

- It includes **foods that require minimal chewing** before swallowing, such as ground meats, canned fruits, and soft-cooked vegetables.

- It excludes harder foods, such as dried fruits, most raw fruits and vegetables, and foods containing seeds and nuts.

- **Indications** for this diet include clients who have limited chewing or swallowing ability; those with dysphagia, poorly fitting dentures, and those who are edentulous (without teeth); those who have had surgery to the head, neck, or mouth; and those with strictures of the intestinal tract.

Δ **Regular Diet (Normal or House Diet)**

- A regular diet is **indicated** for clients who do not need dietary restrictions. They are adjusted to meet age-specific needs throughout the life cycle.

- Many healthcare facilities offer self-select menus for regular diets.

- Dietary modifications to accommodate individual preferences, food habits, and ethnic values can be done without difficulty for the client receiving a regular diet.

Nursing Assessments/Data Collection and Interventions

Δ **Ongoing assessment parameters** include daily weights, ordered laboratory values, and an evaluation of a client's nutritional and energy needs and response to diet therapy.

Δ A client's **nutritional intake** should be observed and documented. A **calorie count** may be performed to determine caloric intake and to evaluate adequacy.

Δ Provide education and support for diet therapy.

Δ **Diet as tolerated** is ordered to permit a client's preferences and ability to eat to be considered. The nurse may assess the client for hunger, appetite, and nausea when planning the most appropriate diet. The nurse should consult with a dietician.

Δ Dietary intake is progressively increased (from nothing by mouth to clear liquids to regular diet) **following major surgeries**. The nurse should assess for the return of bowel function (as evidenced by auscultation of bowel sounds and the passage of flatus) before advancing a client's diet.

Δ A nurse can **increase a client's satisfaction** with a hospital diet through courteous delivery, assistance with the tray, displaying a positive attitude toward the diet and food, and providing education and explanation of the diet.

Primary Reference:

Dudek, S. G. (2006). *Nutrition essentials for nursing practice* (5th ed.). Philadelphia: Lippincott Williams & Wilkins.

Additional Resources:

Stanfield, P., & Hui, Y. H. (2003). *Nutrition and diet therapy: Self-instructional modules.* Sudbury, MA: Jones & Bartlett.

Chapter 12: Hospital Diets

Application Exercises

Scenario: A 54-year-old female client has just returned to her hospital room following an appendectomy (removal of the appendix). She states that she is hungry, and the provider order reads "advance diet as tolerated."

1. Which of the following snacks are appropriate for the client? (Check all that apply.)

     _____ Applesauce

     _____ Cheese and crackers

     _____ Chicken broth

     _____ Sherbet

     _____ Peanut butter sandwich

     _____ Cranberry juice

2. The next day, the client states that she is ready to eat something more substantial. What assessment data is important to obtain before advancing the client's diet?

3. **True or False:** Mechanical soft diets cannot meet the nutritional requirements for clients.

4. **True or False:** Clear liquid diets should not be used for more than 2 to 3 days.

5. **True or False:** A soft or low-fiber diet is appropriate for a client with acute gastritis.

6. **True or False:** Monitoring a client's weight is necessary to determine if nutrition is adequate.

7. A client has been admitted to the hospital with a diagnosis of acute gastritis. He states that he is starving because he hasn't eaten anything all day. The provider order reads for clear liquids only. The client states that he doesn't want the broth and gelatin that is on his dinner tray. What actions should the nurse take?

8. A client is prescribed a full liquid diet with a minimal caloric requirement. Dietary services performed a calorie count, and it showed that the caloric requirements were not being met with the current diet offerings. List some examples of what could be done to meet the client's current caloric needs without diet progression.

Chapter 12: Hospital Diets

Application Exercises Answer Key

Scenario: A 54-year-old female client has just returned to her hospital room following an appendectomy (removal of the appendix). She states that she is hungry, and the provider order reads "advance diet as tolerated."

1. Which of the following snacks are appropriate for the client? (Check all that apply.)

   _____ Applesauce

   _____ Cheese and crackers

   __x__ Chicken broth

   _____ Sherbet

   _____ Peanut butter sandwich

   __x__ Cranberry juice

   Clear liquids are an appropriate choice for a postoperative patient. If these choices are tolerated well by the client, then the diet should progress to full liquids and eventually solid foods.

2. The next day, the client states that she is ready to eat something more substantial. What assessment data is important to obtain before advancing the client's diet?

   Dietary intake should be progressively increased following major surgeries once the return of bowel function has occurred. Therefore, the nurse should verify the client's bowel sounds and presence of gas or flatus. When diet as tolerated is ordered, the nurse should assess the client for hunger, appetite, and nausea when planning the diet. The nurse should also work in conjunction with a dietician when possible.

3. **True or False:** Mechanical soft diets cannot meet the nutritional requirements for clients.

   False: A mechanical soft diet is a regular diet that has been modified for texture. The foods comprising the diet can be modified to meet specific nutrient needs for the client.

4. **True or False:** Clear liquid diets should not be used for more than 2 to 3 days.

   True

5. **True or False:** A soft or low-fiber diet is appropriate for a client with acute gastritis.

   True

6. **True or False:** Monitoring a client's weight is necessary to determine if nutrition is adequate.

   True

7. A client has been admitted to the hospital with a diagnosis of acute gastritis. He states that he is starving because he hasn't eaten anything all day. The provider order reads for clear liquids only. The client states that he doesn't want the broth and gelatin that is on his dinner tray. What actions should the nurse take?

   The nurse should first acknowledge the client's frustration and then explain to him that clear liquid diets are used for clients with acute gastrointestinal disorders because the foods included require minimal digestion and are non-gas forming. Reassure the client that he will be continually assessed and that his diet will be advanced when it is deemed appropriate. It may be helpful to ask the client about his preferences for the clear liquid choices so that he feels involved in his care.

8. A client is prescribed a full liquid diet with a minimal caloric requirement. Dietary services performed a calorie count, and it showed that the caloric requirements were not being met with the current diet offerings. List some examples of what could be done to meet the client's current caloric needs without diet progression.

   Pureed diets can fully meet a client's nutritional needs. Substituting liquids for water when preparing the foods can provide additional calories and nutritional value. Examples include: broth, milk, cream, soup, tomato sauce, or fruit juice. Providing nutritional supplements is another option that will allow the client to obtain adequate caloric and nutrient intake.

Unit 3   Clinical Nutrition and Therapeutic Diets

Chapter 13:   Enteral Nutrition
                Contributor: Jackie H. Jones, EdD, RN

⟳ NCLEX® Connections:

Learning Objective: Review and apply knowledge within "**Enteral Nutrition**" in readiness for performance of the following nutrition nursing activities as outlined by the NCLEX® test plans:

Δ   Verify the placement and patency of the client's feeding tube.

Δ   Evaluate and/or monitor side effects of client tube feedings (diarrhea, dehydration) and intervene as needed.

Δ   Provide care – including initiation, maintenance, and discontinuation – to the client receiving a tube feeding.

Δ   Monitor the hydration status (intake and output, edema, symptoms of dehydration) of the client receiving enteral nutrition.

Δ   Monitor the client's weight to verify that nutritional goals are met by enteral nutrition.

Δ   Utilize measures (small feedings, tube feedings) to enhance the client's nutritional intake.

📖 Key Points

Δ   **Enteral nutrition** (EN) is used when the client cannot consume adequate nutrients and calories orally, but maintains at least **a partially functional gastrointestinal system**.

Δ   Enteral nutrition consists of **blenderized foods** or a **commercial formula administered by a tube** into the **stomach or small intestine**. Enteral feeding most closely utilizes the body's own digestive and metabolic routes.

Enteral Feeding Routes

Δ A client's medical status and the anticipated length of time that tube feeding will be required determine the **type of tube** used.

- **Transnasal tubes** extend from the nose to either the stomach or small intestine.

  ◊ Nasogastric (NG) tubes are passed from the nose to the stomach.

  ◊ Nasointestinal tubes go from the nose to the intestine.

  ◊ These tubes are used short term (usually less than 3 to 4 weeks).

- An **ostomy** is a surgically created opening (**stoma**) made to deliver feedings directly into the stomach or intestines.

  ◊ Gastrostomy tubes are endoscopically or surgically inserted into the stomach.

  ◊ Jejunostomy tubes are surgically inserted into the jejunal portion of the small intestine (jejunum).

Δ **Endoscopic or surgical placement** is preferred when **long-term use** is anticipated or when a nasal obstruction makes insertion through the nose impossible.

Δ Placement into the stomach stimulates normal gastrointestinal function.

Enteral Feeding Formulas

Δ **Commercial products are preferred** over home-blended ingredients because they provide a known nutrient composition, controlled consistency, and bacteriological safety.

Δ **Standard** and **hydrolyzed** formulas are the **two primary types** of enteral feeding formulas available. They are categorized by the complexity of the proteins included.

- **Standard**, also called polymeric or intact, formulas are **composed of whole proteins or protein isolates**.

  ◊ These formulas require a functioning gastrointestinal tract.

  ◊ Most provide 1.0 to 1.2 cal/mL, but are also available in high-protein, high-calorie, and disease-specific formulas.

- **Hydrolyzed**, or elemental, formulas are **composed of free amino acids**.

  ◊ These formulas are used for clients with a partially functioning gastrointestinal tract or those who have an impaired ability to digest and absorb foods. Examples include people with inflammatory bowel disease, short-gut syndrome, cystic fibrosis, and pancreatic disorders.

  ◊ Most formulas provide 1.0 to 1.5 cal/mL. Partially hydrolyzed formulas also provide other nutrients in simpler forms that require little or no digestion.

Δ   Tube feedings may be packaged in **cans** or in **pre-filled bags**.

- Pre-filled bags should be discarded every 24 hr, or per institution policy, even if they are not empty.

- Cans may be used to add formula to a generic bag to infuse via a pump, or for feedings directly from a syringe.

Δ   Other factors to consider in determining an appropriate formula include:

- Caloric density.

- Water content.

- Protein density.

- Osmolality.

- Fiber and residue content.

- Presence of other nutrients.

Enteral Feeding Delivery Methods

Δ   The **delivery method** is dependent on the type and location of the feeding tube, the type of formula being administered, and the client's tolerance.

- **Continuous drip method:** Formula is administered at a continuous rate over a 16- to 24-hr period.

  ◊   **Infusion pumps** help ensure consistent flow rates.

  ◊   This method is recommended for **critically ill clients** because of its association with smaller residual volumes and a lower risk of aspiration and diarrhea.

  ◊   **Residual volumes** should be measured every 4 to 6 hr.

  ◊   Feeding tubes should be flushed with water every 4 hr to maintain patency.

- **Cyclic feedings:** Formula is administered at a continuous rate over an 8- to 16-hr time period, often during sleeping hours.

  ◊   Often used for **transition** from total EN to oral intake.

- **Intermittent tube feedings:** Formula is administered every 4 to 6 hr in equal portions of 200 to 300 mL over a 30- to 60-min time frame.

  ◊   Often used for noncritical clients, home-tube feedings, and clients in rehabilitation.

- **Bolus feedings:** A large volume of formula (500 mL maximum; usual volume is 250 to 400 mL) is administered over a short period of time, usually less than 15 min, four to six times daily.

  ◊   Bolus feedings are delivered directly into the stomach only.

Enteral Feeding Complications

Δ   **Gastrointestinal complications** include:

- Constipation, diarrhea, cramping, pain, abdominal distention, dumping syndrome, nausea, and vomiting.

Δ   **Mechanical complications** include:

- Tube misplacement or dislodgement.

- Aspiration.

- Tube obstruction or rupture. (Feeding tube obstruction can be prevented with flushing of the tube with 20 to 60 mL of warm water after use and every 4 hr and by avoiding dry products and medications.)

- Irritation and leakage at the insertion site and irritation of the nose, esophagus, and mucosa.

Δ   **Metabolic complications** include:

- Dehydration.

- Hyperglycemia.

- Electrolyte imbalances.

- Overhydration.

Δ   **Bacterial contamination** of formula can result in food poisoning.

Δ   Gastrostomy tube feedings are generally well tolerated because the stomach chamber holds and releases feedings in a physiologic manner that promotes more effective digestion. As a result, dumping syndrome is usually avoided.

Nursing Assessments/Data Collection and Interventions

Δ   Prior to instilling enteral feeding, **tube placement** should be **verified by radiography**. Aspirating gastric contents and measuring pH levels are less reliable methods of verifying placement.

Δ   Verify the presence of **bowel sounds**.

Δ   To maintain **feeding tube patency**, it should be **flushed routinely** with warm water.

- **Gastric residuals** should be checked every 4 to 6 hr. If the residual volume exceeds the amount of formula given in the previous 2 hr, then it may be necessary to consider reducing the rate of feeding. **Residuals** should be **returned to the stomach** as they contain electrolytes, nutrients, and digestive enzymes.

Δ The **head of the bed** should be **elevated** at least 30 to 45° during feedings and for at least 30 min afterward to lessen the risk of aspiration.

Δ Begin with a small volume of full-strength formula. Increase volume in intervals as tolerated until the desired volume is achieved.

Δ To avoid **bacterial contamination**:

- Wash hands before handling formula or enteral products.

- Clean equipment and tops of formula cans.

- Cover and label unused cans with the client's name and room number and the date and time of opening.

- Refrigerate unused portions promptly for up to 24 hr.

- Replace the feeding bag and tubing every 24 hr.

- Fill generic bags with less than 6 hr worth of formula.

Δ Administer the feeding solution at **room temperature** to decrease gastrointestinal discomfort.

Δ **Baseline assessment** parameters include:

- Obtain height, weight, and body mass index (BMI).

- Monitor serum albumin, hemoglobin, hematocrit, glucose, and electrolyte levels.

- Evaluate the client's nutritional and energy needs.

- Verify appropriate gastrointestinal function. Dysfunction of the gastrointestinal tract may indicate a need for alternate forms of nutrition.

Δ **Ongoing monitoring** includes:

- Monitor daily weights and daily intake and output.

- Obtain gastric residuals (every 4 to 6 hr).

- Monitor electrolyte levels, BUN, creatinine, serum minerals, and complete blood count (CBC) as prescribed.

- Monitor the tube site for signs and symptoms of infection or intolerance (pain, redness, swelling, drainage).

- Monitor the character and frequency of bowel movements.

Δ **Medications** may be administered through a feeding tube.

- Feeding should be stopped prior to administering medications.

- The tubing should be flushed with water (15 to 30 mL) before and after the medication is given and between each medication if more than one is given.

- Liquid medications should be used when possible.

Δ   **Weaning** occurs as oral consumption increases. Enteral feedings may be discontinued when the client consumes two-thirds of protein and calorie needs orally for 3 to 5 days.

Δ   The client who is **nothing by mouth (NPO)** will require meticulous oral care.

Δ   Some clients may require nutritional support service at home for **long-term enteral nutrition**. A multidisciplinary team, including the nurse, dietician, pharmacist, and primary care provider, monitors the weight, electrolyte balance, and overall physical condition of clients discharged with this type of nutritional therapy.

Primary Reference:

Dudek, S. G. (2006). *Nutrition essentials for nursing practice* (5th ed.). Philadelphia: Lippincott Williams & Wilkins.

Additional Resources:

Hogan, M. A., & Wane, D. (2003). *Nutrition and diet therapy: Reviews and rationales*. Upper Saddle River, NJ: Prentice Hall.

Chapter 13: Enteral Nutrition

Application Exercises

Scenario: A nurse is caring for a client who is receiving mechanical ventilation following a recent surgery. The client has a previously placed nasogastric (NG) tube from another institution. The provider order reads to initiate enteral feedings via the NG tube.

1. What data is important to collect before initiating feedings?

2. The enteral tube feeding began at 1000, and it has been infusing at a continuous rate of 40 mL/hr. It is now 1400. What actions should the nurse perform? Include rationale.

3. What assessment data should the nurse obtain for the ongoing assessment of an enterally fed client?

4. **True or False:** All stomach residual volumes should be discarded to prevent nausea and vomiting.

5. **True or False:** Tube feeding should be administered at room temperature to prevent abdominal cramping.

6. **True or False:** Intermittent tube feedings are typically used for critically ill clients.

7. Which of the following actions are important in the prevention of bacterial contamination of tube feeding? (Check all that apply.)

_____ Fill the generic bag with 24 hr worth of formula from cans.

_____ Wash hands thoroughly.

_____ Leave unused portions in the patient room to avoid cross-contamination.

_____ Cover and label any unused portion with the client name, room number, date, and the time opened.

_____ Replace tubing and feeding bag every 48 hr.

8. A nurse is preparing a client's 0900 medications. The nurse is to administer 11 separate pills through the client's percutaneous endoscopic gastrostomy (PEG) tube. What actions are appropriate for the nurse to perform?

Chapter 13: Enteral Nutrition

Application Exercises Answer Key

Scenario: A nurse is caring for a client who is receiving mechanical ventilation following a recent surgery. The client has a previously placed nasogastric (NG) tube from another institution. The provider order reads to initiate enteral feedings via the NG tube.

1. What data is important to collect before initiating feedings?

The nurse should first verify the presence of bowel sounds in the client. Then, the placement of the tube should be verified by radiography. Measuring pH levels and aspirating gastric contents are less reliable methods of verifying placement. The nurse should elevate the head of the bed to 30 to 45° both during and for 30 to 45 min following the feeding. This is done to reduce the risk of aspiration. Lastly, the nurse should obtain baseline assessment data including height, weight, and BMI. Preliminary laboratory values include albumin, hemoglobin, hematocrit, glucose, and electrolyte levels.

2. The enteral tube feeding began at 1000, and it has been infusing at a continuous rate of 40 mL/hr. It is now 1400. What actions should the nurse perform? Include rationale.

Feeding tubes should be flushed with 20 to 60 mL of warm water every 4 hr to maintain patency. Residuals should be checked every 4 to 6 hr. Performing both of these tasks at the same time allows for less interruption for the client.

3. What assessment data should the nurse obtain for the ongoing assessment of an enterally fed client?

Clients undergoing enteral feedings require careful monitoring to determine the adequacy of the nutrition being received. The nurse should monitor daily weights and intake and output. The frequency and consistency of bowel movements should be included in output measurements. Serum albumin, hemoglobin, hematocrit, glucose, and electrolyte levels are all indicators of nutritional status and should be monitored. Feeding tube sites, whether transnasal or surgical, can be sources of irritation or infection for the client. The nurse should monitor the site for any redness, swelling, pain, or drainage and report it to the provider.

4. **True or False:** All stomach residual volumes should be discarded to prevent nausea and vomiting.

   False: Stomach residual volumes should always be returned because they contain valuable electrolytes, nutrients, and enzymes necessary for digestion.

5. **True or False:** Tube feeding should be administered at room temperature to prevent abdominal cramping.

   True

6. **True or False:** Intermittent tube feedings are typically used for critically ill clients.

   False: Continuous feedings are generally used for critically ill clients, as they are associated with smaller residual volumes and a lower risk of aspiration and diarrhea. Intermittent feedings are often used for non-critical clients, home tube feedings, and those clients in rehabilitation.

7. Which of the following actions are important in the prevention of bacterial contamination of tube feeding? (Check all that apply.)

   _____ Fill the generic bag with 24 hr worth of formula from cans.

   __x__ Wash hands thoroughly.

   _____ Leave unused portions in the patient room to avoid cross-contamination.

   __x__ Cover and label any unused portion with the client name, room number, date, and the time opened.

   _____ Replace tubing and feeding bag every 48 hr.

   Feeding bags should be filled with no more than 6 hr worth of formula. Pre-filled bags usually contain enough formula for a 24-hr period. Any unused portion should be covered, properly labeled, and refrigerated. Tubing and feeding should be replaced every 24 hr unless otherwise specified by institution policy.

8. A nurse is preparing a client's 0900 medications. The nurse is to administer 11 separate pills through the client's percutaneous endoscopic gastrostomy (PEG) tube. What actions are appropriate for the nurse to perform?

Medications may be administered through a feeding tube, but they do pose a risk for tube obstruction. The nurse should first check with the pharmacist to determine what medications may be available in liquid form. Pills should be thoroughly crushed and diluted before administering them. The tube feeding should be stopped before administering the medications. The tube should be flushed with water (15 to 30 mL) before and after each medication.

Unit 3   Clinical Nutrition and Therapeutic Diets

Chapter 14:   Parenteral Nutrition
Contributor: Jackie H. Jones, EdD, RN

⟳ NCLEX® Connections:

Learning Objective: Review and apply knowledge within "**Parenteral Nutrition**" in readiness for performance of the following nutrition nursing activities as outlined by the NCLEX® test plans:

Δ   Evaluate and/or monitor side effects of parenteral nutrition and intervene as needed.

Δ   Provide care – including initiation, maintenance, and discontinuation – to the client receiving a tube feeding.

Δ   Monitor the hydration status (intake and output, edema, symptoms of dehydration) of the client receiving parenteral nutrition.

Δ   Monitor the client's weight to verify that nutritional goals are met by parenteral nutrition.

📖 Key Points

Δ   **Parenteral nutrition (PN)** is used when a client's gastrointestinal tract is not functioning or when a client cannot, for either physical or psychological reasons, consume sufficient nutrients orally or enterally.

Δ   Based upon the client's nutritional needs and anticipated duration of therapy, PN can be given as either **total parenteral nutrition (TPN)** or **peripheral parenteral nutrition (PPN)**.

Δ   **TPN** provides a nutritionally complete solution and can be used **when caloric needs are very high** (more than 2,500 cal/day), when the anticipated **duration of therapy is greater than 7 days**, or when the solution to be administered is hypertonic (composed of greater than 10% dextrose). *It can only be administered in a central vein.*

Δ   **TPN** is commonly used in clients undergoing **treatment for cancer** and those suffering from **trauma** or **extensive burns** because these conditions are associated with high caloric requirements.

△ **PPN** can provide a nutritionally complete solution; however, because it is administered into a peripheral vein, the **nutritional value is limited**. The solution must be **isotonic** and contain **less than 10% dextrose and 5% amino acids**.

△ **PPN** may be used when central venous access is not available or for transition from TPN to enteral or oral intake. It is appropriate for use when parenteral nutrition is needed for **less than 7 days** or when **caloric needs** are **less than 2,500 cal/day**.

Components of Parenteral Nutrition Solutions

△ PN includes **amino acids, dextrose, electrolytes, vitamins,** and **trace elements** in **sterile water**.

△ **Lipid emulsions** may be added to the solution, administered "**piggyback**" (a secondary infusion), or given intermittently.

△ **Carbohydrate or dextrose solutions** are available in concentrations of 5 to 70%. To avoid hyperglycemia and other complications, dextrose infusions should not exceed 4 to 5 mg/kg/min.

△ **Protein** is provided as a mixture of essential and non-essential amino acids and is available in concentrations of 3 to 15%.

• Protein should provide 10 to 20% of total calorie intake.

• The client's estimated requirements and hepatic and renal function determine the amount of protein provided.

△ Electrolytes, vitamins, and trace elements are essential for normal body functions. The amounts added depend upon the client's blood chemistry values, and physical assessment findings are used to determine the quantity of electrolytes.

△ **Lipids (fats)** are available in concentrations of 10, 20, and 30%. Lipids are a significant source of calories, and they are used to correct or prevent essential fatty acid deficiency.

• **Lipid emulsions** may be added to the solution, administered piggyback, or may be given intermittently. Intravenous lipids are **contraindicated** for clients who have **hyperlipidemia** or severe hepatic disease.

△ **Medications may be added** to parenteral nutrition. They should be added by the pharmacist to avoid incompatibilities. Insulin may be added to reduce the potential for hyperglycemia. Heparin is sometimes added to prevent fibrin buildup on the catheter tip.

Nursing Assessments/Data Collection and Interventions

Δ   Nursing care is focused on preventing complications through **consistent monitoring**. Specific monitoring guidelines vary among healthcare facilities.

Δ   **Prior to initiating PN**, the nurse should review the client's weight, BMI, nutritional status, diagnosis, and current laboratory data, which may include: complete blood count (CBC), serum chemistry profile, prothrombin time and partial thromboplastin time (PT/PTT), iron, total iron-binding capacity, lipid profile, liver function tests, electrolyte panel, and BUN.

Δ   The nurse should also assess the client's **educational needs**.

Δ   **Strict aseptic techniques** are maintained to reduce the risk of infection. The high dextrose content of PN contributes to bacterial growth.

Δ   Use sterile technique when **changing central line dressing and tubing**. The bag and tubing should be changed every 24 hr.

Δ   **Monitor serum** and **urine glucose** as prescribed. Sliding scale insulin may be prescribed to intervene for hyperglycemia.

Δ   **Ongoing assessment parameters** include: intake and output, daily weights, vital signs, pertinent laboratory values, and ongoing evaluation of the client's underlying condition. This data is used to determine the client's response to therapy and the formulation of the solution to prevent nutrient deficiencies or toxicities.

Δ   Evidence supporting the effectiveness of parenteral nutrition includes:

•   **Daily weight gain** of up to 1 kg/day.

•   **Increases** in **albumin** level (normal 3.5 to 5.5 g/dL) and in **prealbumin** level (normal 23 to 43 mg/dL).

Δ   **Flow rate** should be monitored carefully:

•   Failure to provide optimal nutritional intake results from solutions administered too slowly.

•   **Hyperosmolar diuresis** can result from too rapid an infusion and can lead to seizures, coma, and death.

Δ   An **electronic infusion device** should be used to prevent accidental overload of solution.

Δ   Monitor for **"cracking" of TPN solution.** This occurs if the calcium or phosphorous content is high or if poor-salt albumin is added. A "cracked" TPN solution has an oily appearance or a layer of fat on top of the solution and should not be used.

Δ   Monitor for signs of **potential complications**:

- **Infection and sepsis**, as evidenced by fever or elevated WBC. Infection can result from contamination of the catheter during insertion, contaminated solution, or a long-term indwelling catheter.

- **Metabolic complications**, which include hyperglycemia, hypoglycemia, hyperkalemia, hypophosphatemia, hypocalcemia, hypoalbuminemia, dehydration, and fluid overload (as evidenced by weight gain greater than 1 kg/day and edema).

- **Mechanical complications,** which include catheter misplacement, pneumothorax (as evidenced by shortness of breath or diminished or absent breath sounds), subclavian artery puncture, catheter embolus, air embolus, thrombosis, obstruction, and bolus infusion.

Δ   PN should be **discontinued as soon as** possible to avoid potential complications, but not until the **client's enteral or oral intake can provide 60%** or more of estimated **caloric requirements**.

Δ   Discontinuance should be done gradually to avoid **rebound hypoglycemia**.

Δ   **Education** for clients regarding **TPN at home** should include aseptic preparation and administration techniques and criteria to monitor signs and symptoms of infection and other complications as highlighted above.

Primary Reference:

Dudek, S. G. (2006). *Nutrition essentials for nursing practice* (5th ed.). Philadelphia: Lippincott Williams & Wilkins.

Additional Resources:

Hogan, M. A., & Wane, D. (2003). *Nutrition and diet therapy: Reviews and rationales.* Upper Saddle River, NJ: Prentice Hall.

Chapter 14: Parenteral Nutrition

Application Exercises

Scenario: A nurse is caring for a client with a paralytic ileus (paralysis of the intestine) who is scheduled to begin receiving PPN.

1. What baseline assessment data should the nurse obtain prior to starting the PPN? What assessment data should be included in the ongoing monitoring of the client?

2. After 48 hr of PPN, the client's blood glucose level is 275 mg/dL. The nurse notifies the provider and receives an order for insulin to be added to the bag of PPN. Describe the appropriate method for adding medications to PPN therapy. Include rationale.

3. The client's PPN bag has arrived from the pharmacy and is due to be changed at 1800. The nurse notices a layer of fat on the top of the solution. What actions should be taken?

4. After 6 days of PPN therapy, the client's bowel sounds have returned and he is consuming 1,500 cal/day via oral intake. What actions should the nurse anticipate?

5. Which of the following criteria should be monitored for a client undergoing PN? (Check all that apply.)

　　　　　_____ Breath sounds

　　　　　_____ Oral intake

　　　　　_____ WBC

　　　　　_____ Electrolytes

　　　　　_____ Vital signs

　　　　　_____ Daily weights

　　　　　_____ Blood glucose

　　　　　_____ Peripheral IV or central line site

6. **True or False:** Lipids should always be administered for a client with PN.

7. **True or False:** TPN solutions should always be administered through a central line.

8. **True or False:** Protein should comprise 10% of all PN solutions to promote muscle building and healing.

9. **True or False:** TPN is preferred for clients expected to receive PN longer than 7 days.

10. A client is scheduled to continue her TPN therapy at home following discharge from the hospital. What information is important to include in her discharge instructions?

Chapter 14: Parenteral Nutrition

Application Exercises Answer Key

Scenario: A nurse is caring for a client with a paralytic ileus (paralysis of the intestine) who is scheduled to begin receiving PPN.

1. What baseline assessment data should the nurse obtain prior to starting the PPN? What assessment data should be included in the ongoing monitoring of the client?

   Prior to beginning any type of PN, the nurse should review the client's weight, BMI, nutritional status, laboratory values, and current medical diagnosis. Once the PN is started, ongoing assessment parameters should include daily intake and output, daily weights, vital signs, laboratory values, and the client's underlying condition. This data is important because it aids the healthcare team in determining the effectiveness of the PN. If any abnormal values are identified, the PN solution can be modified to address the deficiencies or excesses.

2. After 48 hr of PPN, the client's blood glucose level is 275 mg/dL. The nurse notifies the provider and receives an order for insulin to be added to the bag of PPN. Describe the appropriate method for adding medications to PPN therapy. Include rationale.

   The nurse should notify the pharmacist responsible for the client's care about the order. Any medications should be added by the pharmacist to avoid any incompatibilities with the PN solution.

3. The client's PPN bag has arrived from the pharmacy and is due to be changed at 1800. The nurse notices a layer of fat on the top of the solution. What actions should be taken?

   The nurse should recognize this as "cracking" of the PPN solution. This can occur if the calcium or phosphorous concentration of the solution is too high or if poor-salt albumin is used. The solution should not be used, and a new solution should be obtained.

4. After 6 days of PPN therapy, the client's bowel sounds have returned and he is consuming 1,500 cal/day via oral intake. What actions should the nurse anticipate?

Any PN should be discontinued as soon as possible to avoid complications such as infection, electrolyte imbalances, or fluid overload. This client is receiving PPN, which is generally recommended for those clients who have caloric needs less than 2,500 cal/day. The nurse should expect the PPN to be discontinued as this client is consuming 1,700 cal/day orally, which is more than the 60% that is recommended for discontinuing PN. It is important to note that discontinuing PN should be done gradually to avoid rebound hypoglycemia.

5. Which of the following criteria should be monitored for a client undergoing PN? (Check all that apply.)

  __x__ Breath sounds

  __x__ Oral intake

  __x__ WBC

  __x__ Electrolytes

  __x__ Vital signs

  __x__ Daily weights

  __x__ Blood glucose

  __x__ Peripheral IV or central line site

6. **True or False:** Lipids should always be administered for a client with PN.

False: Lipids are contraindicated for clients with hyperlipidemia or severe hepatic disease.

7. **True or False:** TPN solutions should always be administered through a central line.

True

8. **True or False:** Protein should comprise 10% of all PN solutions to promote muscle building and healing.

False: Protein should provide 10 to 20% of calories, but a client's individual requirements, hepatic function, and renal function are the determining factors for the amount of protein added.

9. **True or False:** TPN is preferred for clients expected to receive PN longer than 7 days.

True

10. A client is scheduled to continue her TPN therapy at home following discharge from the hospital. What information is important to include in her discharge instructions?

It is important to instruct the client on aseptic preparation and sterile technique for administering the solution and changing the dressing. The nurse should also teach the client about common complications of TPN (infection, fluid overload, dehydration, hyperglycemia) and their respective signs and symptoms.

Unit 3   Clinical Nutrition and Therapeutic Diets

Chapter 15:   Nutrition for Clients with Gastrointestinal Disorders

Contributor: Pamela Y. Mahon, PhD, RN

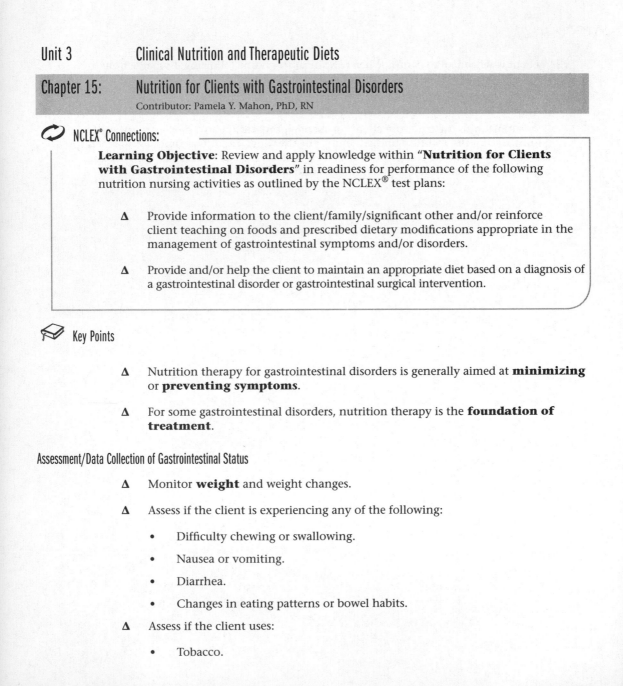

NCLEX® Connections:

Learning Objective: Review and apply knowledge within "**Nutrition for Clients with Gastrointestinal Disorders**" in readiness for performance of the following nutrition nursing activities as outlined by the NCLEX® test plans:

Δ   Provide information to the client/family/significant other and/or reinforce client teaching on foods and prescribed dietary modifications appropriate in the management of gastrointestinal symptoms and/or disorders.

Δ   Provide and/or help the client to maintain an appropriate diet based on a diagnosis of a gastrointestinal disorder or gastrointestinal surgical intervention.

Key Points

Δ   Nutrition therapy for gastrointestinal disorders is generally aimed at **minimizing** or **preventing symptoms**.

Δ   For some gastrointestinal disorders, nutrition therapy is the **foundation of treatment**.

Assessment/Data Collection of Gastrointestinal Status

Δ   Monitor **weight** and weight changes.

Δ   Assess if the client is experiencing any of the following:

• Difficulty chewing or swallowing.

• Nausea or vomiting.

• Diarrhea.

• Changes in eating patterns or bowel habits.

Δ   Assess if the client uses:

• Tobacco.

- Alcohol.

- Caffeine.

- Over-the-counter medications for gastrointestinal symptoms.

- Nutritional supplements.

Δ Monitor for **abnormal laboratory values**.

Δ Monitor **bowel sounds**.

Common Diet Strategies

Δ **Low-fiber diets** avoid foods that are high in residue content, such as whole-grain breads and cereals and raw fruits and vegetables.

- Diets low in fiber reduce the frequency and volume of **fecal output** and slow transit time of food through the digestive tract.

- Low-fiber diets are used short term for:

  ◊ Diarrhea.

  ◊ Acute diverticulitis.

  ◊ Malabsorption syndromes.

  ◊ Preparation for bowel surgery.

Δ **High-fiber diets** focus on foods that contain **more than 5 g** of fiber **per serving**. A diet high in fiber helps:

- Increase stool bulk.

- Stimulate peristalsis.

- Prevent constipation.

- Protect against colon cancer.

Common Gastrointestinal Disorders and Nursing Interventions

Δ **Anorexia**

- Anorexia is defined as a lack of appetite. It is not the same as anorexia nervosa.

- **Provide small, frequent meals** and **avoid high-fat foods** to help maximize the intake of clients who are anorexic.

Δ **Nausea and Vomiting**

- **Potential causes** of nausea and vomiting include: decreased gastric acid secretion; decreased gastrointestinal motility; bacterial or vital infection; increased intracranial pressure; liver, pancreatic, and gall bladder disorders; or side effects of some medications.

- The underlying cause of the nausea and vomiting should be investigated.

- Once the client's symptoms subside, **begin with clear liquids** followed by full liquids and then advance the diet as tolerated.

- **Low-fat carbohydrate foods,** such as crackers, toast, oatmeal, and bland fruit, are usually well tolerated.

- **Other interventions** include:

  ◊ Clients should avoid liquids with meals because they promote a feeling of fullness.

  ◊ Promote good oral hygiene with mouthwash and ice chips.

  ◊ Elevate the head of the bed.

  ◊ Discourage heated and spicy foods.

Δ **Constipation**

- Constipation is **difficult** or **infrequent passage of stools**, which may be hard and dry.

- **Causes** include: irregular bowel habits, psychogenic factors, inactivity, chronic laxative use or abuse, obstruction, medications, and inadequate consumption of fiber and fluid.

- Encouraging **exercise** and a diet **high** in **fiber** and promoting **adequate fluid intake** may help alleviate symptoms.

Δ **Dysphagia**

- Dysphagia is an alteration in the client's **ability to swallow**.

- **Causes** include: obstruction, inflammation, edema, and certain neurological disorders.

- Modifying the **texture** of **foods** and the **consistency** of **liquids** may enable the client to achieve proper nutrition.

- Clients with dysphagia are at an **increased risk of aspiration**. Place the client in an **upright or high-Fowler's position** to facilitate swallowing.

- Provide **oral care** prior to eating to enhance the client's sense of taste.

- Allow adequate time for eating, utilize adaptive eating devices, and encourage small bites and thorough chewing.

- Avoid thin liquids and sticky foods.

- **Nutritional supplements** may be indicated if nutritional intake is deemed inadequate.

Δ **Dumping Syndrome**

- This occurs as a **complication of gastric surgeries** that inhibit the ability of the **pyloric sphincter** to control the movement of food into the small intestine.

  ◊ This "dumping" results in nausea, distention, cramping pains, and diarrhea within 15 min after eating.

  ◊ Weakness, dizziness, a rapid heartbeat, and hypoglycemia may occur.

- **Small, frequent meals** are indicated.

- Consumption of **protein** and **fat** at each meal is indicated.

- Avoid concentrated **sugars**.

- Restrict **lactose** intake.

- Consume liquids 1 hr before or after eating instead of with meals (**dry diet**).

Δ **Gastroesophageal Reflux Disease (GERD)**

- GERD leads to **indigestion** and **heartburn** from the backflow of acidic gastric juices onto the mucosa of the lower esophagus.

- Encourage **weight loss** for overweight clients.

- Avoid large meals and bedtime snacks.

- Avoid **trigger foods** such as citrus fruits and juices, spicy foods, and carbonated beverages.

- Avoid items that reduce **lower esophageal sphincter (LES) pressure**, including:

  ◊ Alcohol.

  ◊ Caffeine.

  ◊ Chocolate.

  ◊ Fatty foods.

  ◊ Peppermint and spearmint flavors.

  ◊ Cigarette smoke.

Δ **Peptic Ulcer Disease (PUD)**

- PUD is characterized by an **erosion** of the **mucosal layer** of the **stomach** or **duodenum**.

- This may be caused by a **bacterial infection** with *Helicobacter pylori* or the **chronic use** of non-steroidal anti-inflammatory drugs (**NSAIDs**), such as aspirin and ibuprofen.

- **Avoid** eating **frequent meals** and **snacks**, as they promote increased gastric acid secretion.

- Avoid alcohol, cigarette smoking, aspirin and other NSAIDs, coffee, black pepper, spicy foods, and caffeine.

Δ **Gastritis**

- Gastritis is characterized by **inflammation** of the **gastric mucosa**.

- **Causes** include food poisoning, radiation therapy, metabolic stress, and excessive alcohol use.

- **Symptoms** include vomiting, bleeding, and hematemesis (vomiting of blood).

- **Avoid** eating **frequent meals** and **snacks**, as they promote increased gastric acid secretion.

- Avoid alcohol, cigarette smoking, aspirin and other NSAIDs, coffee, black pepper, spicy foods, and caffeine.

Δ **Lactose Intolerance**

- Lactose intolerance results from an **inadequate supply of lactase**, the enzyme that digests lactose.

- **Symptoms** include distention, cramps, flatus, and diarrhea.

- Clients should be encouraged to avoid or limit their intake of foods high in lactose such as: milk, sour cream, cheese, cream soups, coffee creamer, chocolate, ice cream, and puddings.

Δ **Ileostomies and Colostomies**

- An **ostomy** is a surgically created opening on the surface of the abdomen from either the end of the **small intestine (ileostomy)** or from the **colon (colostomy)**.

- **Fluid** and **electrolyte maintenance** is the primary concern for clients with ileostomies and colostomies.

- The colon absorbs large amounts of **fluid, sodium,** and **potassium**.

- Nutrition therapy **begins with liquids** only, and then the diet is slowly advanced based upon client tolerance.

- Advise the client to consume a diet that is **high in fluids and soluble fiber**.

- Encourage the client to **avoid foods** that **cause gas** (beans, eggs, carbonated beverages) and **stomal blockage** (nuts, raw carrots, popcorn).

- Additional **calories** and **protein** are needed to **promote healing** of the stoma site.

- These clients require emotional support due to their **altered body image**.

Δ **Diverticulosis and Diverticulitis**

- **Diverticula** are pouches that protrude from the wall of the intestine.

- **Diverticulosis** is a condition characterized by the presence of diverticula.

- **Diverticulitis** is the inflammation that occurs when fecal matter becomes trapped in the diverticula.

- A **high-fiber diet** may prevent diverticulosis and diverticulitis by producing stools that are easily passed and thus decreasing pressure within the colon.

- During **acute diverticulitis**, a low-fiber diet is prescribed in order to reduce bowel stimulation.

- **Avoid** foods with **seeds** or **husks**.

- Clients require instruction regarding diet adjustment based on the need for an acute intervention or preventive approach.

Δ **Inflammatory Bowel Disease**

- **Crohn's disease** (regional enteritis) and **ulcerative colitis** are chronic, inflammatory bowel diseases characterized by periods of exacerbation and remission.

- **Symptoms** include nausea, vomiting, weight loss, crampy abdominal pain, fever, fatigue, and anorexia.

- Nutrition therapy is focused on providing nutrients in forms that the client can tolerate.

Δ **Cholecystitis**

- Cholecystitis is characterized by **inflammation of the gallbladder**.

- The gallbladder stores and releases bile that aids in the digestion of fats.

- **Fat intake should be limited** to reduce stimulation of the gallbladder.

- Other foods that may cause problems include coffee, broccoli, cauliflower, Brussels sprouts, cabbage, onions, legumes, and highly seasoned foods.

- Otherwise, the diet is individualized to the client's needs and tolerance.

Δ **Pancreatitis**

- Pancreatitis is an **inflammation of the pancreas**.

- The pancreas is responsible for secreting enzymes needed to digest fats, carbohydrates, and proteins.

- Nutritional therapy for acute pancreatitis involves **reducing any pancreatic stimulation.** Therefore, the client is nothing by mouth (NPO).

- **Total parenteral nutrition (TPN)** may be used until oral intake may be resumed.

- Nutritional therapy for **chronic pancreatitis** usually includes a low-fat, high-protein, high-carbohydrate diet.

Δ **Liver Disease**

- The liver is involved in the **metabolism** of almost all nutrients.

- **Malnutrition** is common with liver disease.

- **Protein needs** are increased to promote a positive nitrogen balance and to prevent breakdown of the body's protein stores.

- **Caloric requirements** may need to be increased based upon an evaluation of the client's stage of disease, weight, and general health status.

- **Multivitamins** (especially vitamins B, C, and K) and **mineral supplements** may be necessary.

- **Alcohol** should be **eliminated**.

Primary Reference:

Dudek, S. G. (2006). *Nutrition essentials for nursing practice* (5th ed.). Philadelphia: Lippincott Williams & Wilkins.

Additional Resources:

Potter, P. A., & Perry, A. G. (2005). *Fundamentals of nursing* (6th ed.). St. Louis, MO: Mosby.

Chapter 15: Nutrition for Clients with Gastrointestinal Disorders

Application Exercises

1. Match the gastrointestinal disorders listed below with the appropriate dietary recommendations.

_____ Dysphagia		A. The client should remain NPO. TPN may be utilized.
_____ GERD		B. Low-fiber diet during the acute phase.
_____ Nausea and vomiting		C. Low-fat diet to decrease stimulation of the gallbladder.
_____ Dumping syndrome		D. High-fiber diet is a preventative measure.
_____ Pancreatitis		E. Increase protein intake to avoid utilizing bodily stores.
_____ Diverticulitis		F. Consider modifying the texture of foods and consistency of liquids.
_____ Cholecystitis		G. Low-fat carbohydrate foods, such as crackers, toast, and oatmeal.
_____ Diverticulosis		H. Small, frequent meals are indicated for this postoperative complication.
_____ Liver disease		I. Avoid large meals, eating late, alcohol, caffeine, and smoking.

2. Provide a summary of the dietary recommendations for clients suffering from gastrointestinal disorders affecting the mucosa of the stomach (PUD and gastritis).

3. What dietary recommendations should a nurse anticipate sharing with a client suffering from inflammatory bowel disease?

Chapter 15: Nutrition for Clients with Gastrointestinal Disorders

Application Exercises Answer Key

1. Match the gastrointestinal disorders listed below with the appropriate dietary recommendations.

__F__ Dysphagia

__I__ GERD

__G__ Nausea and vomiting

__H__ Dumping Syndrome

__A__ Pancreatitis

__B__ Diverticulitis

__C__ Cholecystitis

__D__ Diverticulosis

__E__ Liver disease

A. The client should remain NPO. TPN may be utilized.

B. Low-fiber diet during the acute phase.

C. Low-fat diet to decrease stimulation of the gallbladder.

D. High-fiber diet is a preventative measure.

E. Increase protein intake to avoid utilizing bodily stores.

F. Consider modifying the texture of foods and consistency of liquids.

G. Low-fat carbohydrate foods, such as crackers, toast, and oatmeal.

H. Small, frequent meals are indicated for this postoperative complication.

I. Avoid large meals, eating late, alcohol, caffeine, and smoking.

2. Provide a summary of the dietary recommendations for clients suffering from gastrointestinal disorders affecting the mucosa of the stomach (PUD and gastritis).

In general, these clients should avoid eating frequent meals as this promotes the secretion of gastric acid, which irritates the affected areas of the mucosa. Clients should also be encouraged to avoid NSAIDs, alcohol, caffeine, smoking, coffee, and spicy foods as these are gastric irritants.

3. What dietary recommendations should a nurse anticipate sharing with a client suffering from inflammatory bowel disease?

Based upon a review of the symptoms associated with inflammatory bowel disease, the client should be encouraged to:

During periods of exacerbation

Δ   **Consume foods low in fiber to minimize bowel stimulation.**

Δ   **Avoid alcohol, caffeine, and cold and carbonated beverages as they are stimulants.**

Δ Consume foods high in protein and calories to restore weight and nutrient deficiencies.

Δ Consume small, frequent meals to help maximize absorption.

During periods of remission

Δ Consume a well-balanced diet that is well tolerated by the client.

Unit 3   Clinical Nutrition and Therapeutic Diets

Chapter 16:   Nutrition for Clients with Cardiovascular Disorders
Contributor: Dana Bartlett, MSN, RN, CSPI

↻ NCLEX® Connections:

Learning Objective: Review and apply knowledge within "**Nutrition for Clients with Cardiovascular Disorders**" in readiness for performance of the following nutrition nursing activities as outlined by the NCLEX® test plans:

Δ   Provide information to the client/family/significant other and/or reinforce client teaching on foods and prescribed dietary modifications in relationship to cardiovascular disease.

Δ   Provide and/or help the client to maintain an appropriate diet based on a diagnosis of cardiovascular disease.

📖 Key Points

Δ   Cardiovascular diseases are the **leading cause of death** in the United States. **Coronary heart disease** (CHD) is the single leading cause of death.

Δ   CHD is caused by **atherosclerosis**, a process of damage and cholesterol deposits on the blood vessels of the heart.

Δ   **Hypercholesterolemia** is a major risk factor for developing CHD.

Δ   High density lipoprotein (**HDL**) cholesterol is the **"good" cholesterol** because it removes cholesterol from the serum and takes it to the liver.

Δ   Low density lipoprotein (**LDL**) cholesterol is the **"bad" cholesterol** because it transports cholesterol out of the liver and into the circulatory system, where it can form plaques on the coronary artery walls.

Δ   Evidence has demonstrated that a diet that is high in cholesterol and saturated fats greatly increases the chances of developing heart disease.

Nutrition Guidelines for the Prevention of Heart Disease

Δ   Consuming **a low-fat, low-cholesterol diet** can reduce the risk of developing CHD.

Δ Daily **cholesterol** intake should be **less than 300 mg**.

Δ Conservative use of **red wine** may reduce the risk of developing CHD.

Δ Increasing fiber and carbohydrate intake, avoiding saturated fat, and decreasing red meat consumption can decrease the risk for developing CHD.

Δ **Homocysteine** is an amino acid. Elevated homocysteine levels can increase the risk of developing CHD. Deficiencies in folate and possibly vitamins B_6 and B_{12} may increase homocysteine levels.

Nursing Interventions for Clients with CHD

Δ Secondary prevention efforts for CHD are focused on **lifestyle changes that lower LDL**. These include a diet low in cholesterol and saturated fats, a diet high in fiber, exercise and weight management, and smoking cessation.

Δ Daily cholesterol intake should be less than 200 mg/day. Saturated fat should be limited to less than 7% of daily caloric intake.

Δ To **lower cholesterol and saturated fats**, instruct the client to:

• Trim visible fat from meats.

• Limit red meats and choose lean meats (turkey, chicken).

• Remove the skin from meats.

• Broil, bake, or steam foods. Avoid frying foods.

• Use low-fat or nonfat milk, cheese, and yogurt.

• Use spices in place of butter or salt to season foods.

• Avoid trans fat as it increases LDL. Partially hydrogenated products contain trans fat.

• Read labels.

Δ Encourage the client to consume a **high-fiber diet**. Soluble fiber lowers LDL.

• Oats, beans, fruits, vegetables, whole grains, barley, and flax are good sources of fiber.

Δ Encourage the client to **exercise**.

• Instruct the client on practical methods for increasing physical activity. For example, encourage them to take the stairs rather than the elevator.

• Provide them with references for local exercise facilities.

Δ Instruct the client to **stop all use of tobacco products**.

Δ The recommended lifestyle changes represent a significant change for many clients.

Δ   Provide support to the client/family/significant other.

Δ   **Encourage significant others to participate** in the changes to ease the transition for the client.

Δ   Explain the rationale as to why the diet is important.

Δ   Aid the client in developing a diet that is complementary to personal **food preferences and lifestyle**. A food diary may be helpful.

Δ   Instruct the client that occasional deviations from the diet are reasonable.

Nutrition Guidelines and Nursing Interventions for Specific Cardiovascular Disorders

Δ   **Hypertension** is a significant risk factor for developing CHD.

- The **DASH diet** is a low-sodium, high-potassium, and high-calcium diet that has proven to lower blood pressure and cholesterol.

  ◊   **Lower sodium intake** (a daily intake of **less than 2,400 mg** is recommended).

  ◊   Foods high in sodium include: canned soups and sauces, potato chips, pretzels, smoked meats, seasonings, and processed foods.

  ◊   Include low-fat dairy products to **promote calcium intake**.

  ◊   Include **fruits** and **vegetables** rich in **potassium** (apricots, bananas, tomatoes, potatoes).

- Limit alcohol intake.

- Encourage the client to read labels and educate the client about appropriate food choices.

- Other **lifestyle changes** include exercising, losing weight, and smoking cessation.

Δ   **Congestive heart failure (CHF)** is a condition in which the heart is not strong enough to pump blood to the periphery. It results in excess sodium and fluid retention and edema. Dietary goals include:

- Reduce **sodium** intake.

- Monitor (and possibly restrict) **fluid intake**.

Δ   After a **myocardial infarction**, it is necessary to reduce the myocardial oxygen demands related to metabolic activity.

- A **liquid diet** is best for the **first 24 hr** after the infarction.

- **Caffeine** should be avoided as it stimulates the heart and increases heart rate.

- **Small, frequent meals** are indicated.

- Counsel the client about the recommendations for a heart-healthy diet.

Primary Reference:

Dudek, S. G. (2006). *Nutrition essentials for nursing practice* (5th ed.). Philadelphia: Lippincott Williams & Wilkins.

Additional Resources:

For more information on a heart-healthy lifestyle, visit the U.S. Food and Drug Administration at: *www.fda.gov/hearthealth/lifestyles/lifestyles.html* or the American Heart Association at: *www.americanheart.org*.

Chapter 16: Nutrition for Clients with Cardiovascular Disorders

Application Exercises

Scenario: A nurse is caring for a client who suffered a myocardial infarction at 0300. The client is taken to the heart catheterization laboratory and undergoes a percutaneous transluminal coronary angioplasty to reduce the blockage in her affected coronary artery.

1. The time is 1200, and the client states that she is hungry. Which of the following food choices are appropriate for this client? (Check all that apply.)

    _____ Low-fat cheese and crackers

    _____ Graham crackers and skim milk

    _____ Reduced-sodium chicken broth

    _____ Cranberry juice

    _____ Turkey sandwich, carrot sticks, and low-fat milk

    _____ Gelatin

    _____ Coffee

2. The client asks, "What is the difference between good cholesterol and bad cholesterol?" How should the nurse respond?

3. The client's spouse has arrived at the hospital to take her home. What information is appropriate to share with the spouse regarding the client's new dietary recommendations?

4. **True or False:** Frying foods is okay as long as they are vegetables and low-fat meats.

5. **True or False:** Trans fats are found in hydrogenated products.

6. **True or False:** Chewing tobacco is an acceptable form of tobacco use for clients.

7. **True or False:** Clients with CHF should increase their fluid intake.

8. Describe the DASH diet and its indications for use.

9. What general dietary recommendations are appropriate for the prevention and control of CHD?

10. List 10 useful tips for clients looking to adopt a heart-healthy lifestyle.

Chapter 16: Nutrition for Clients with Cardiovascular Disorders

Application Exercises Answer Key

Scenario: A nurse is caring for a client who suffered a myocardial infarction at 0300. The client is taken to the heart catheterization laboratory and undergoes a percutaneous transluminal coronary angioplasty to reduce the blockage in her affected coronary artery.

1. The time is 1200, and the client states that she is hungry. Which of the following food choices are appropriate for this client? (Check all that apply.)

      _____ Low-fat cheese and crackers

      _____ Graham crackers and skim milk

      __x__ Reduced-sodium chicken broth

      __x__ Cranberry juice

      _____ Turkey sandwich, carrot sticks, and low-fat milk

      __x__ Gelatin

      _____ Coffee

2. The client asks, "What is the difference between good cholesterol and bad cholesterol?" How should the nurse respond?

The nurse should explain that good cholesterol is known as HDL. It removes cholesterol from the bloodstream and transports it to the liver. LDL is known as bad cholesterol. LDL transports cholesterol into the bloodstream where it is readily available to form artery plaques (atherosclerosis).

3. The client's spouse has arrived at the hospital to take her home. What information is appropriate to share with the spouse regarding the client's new dietary recommendations?

The nurse should review all of the dietary and lifestyle recommendations with the client and her spouse. The nurse should then encourage the spouse to participate in the client's new lifestyle in order to ease the transition for the client. Lastly, the nurse should support the client and her spouse and acknowledge that the recommendations may be a significant change for them. Explain why the modifications are necessary and reassure them that occasional deviations from the diet are acceptable.

4. **True or False:** Frying foods is okay as long as they are vegetables and low-fat meats.

False: Clients should be encouraged to broil, bake, or steam foods to decrease fat content.

5. **True or False:** Trans fats are found in hydrogenated products.

True

6. **True or False:** Chewing tobacco is an acceptable form of tobacco use for clients.

False: All forms of tobacco use should be discontinued.

7. **True or False:** Clients with CHF should increase their fluid intake.

False: Clients should restrict fluid intake with CHF because fluid retention and edema are complications of CHF.

8. Describe the DASH diet and its indications for use.

The DASH diet is a low-sodium, high-potassium, high-calcium diet that aids in the lowering of blood pressure and cholesterol. Clients should restrict their sodium intake to less than 2,400 mg/day. Avoiding canned soups and sauces and salty snacks (potato chips, smoked meats, processed foods) contributes to lower sodium consumption. Tomatoes, bananas, and apricots are examples of high-potassium foods. Calcium sources should be from low-fat dairy products and other calcium-fortified foods. Reading labels will aid the client in identifying the appropriate food choices.

9. What general dietary recommendations are appropriate for the prevention and control of CHD?

In general, clients should consume a diet that is low in fat (especially saturated fats) low in sodium, and low in cholesterol. High-fiber foods also positively contribute to cardiac health. Red wine can be consumed in moderation. Clients should also be encouraged to maintain a healthy weight, exercise, and discontinue tobacco use.

10. List 10 useful tips for clients looking to adopt a heart-healthy lifestyle.

Examples include:

> Trim the fat from meats.
> Bake, broil, and steam foods.
> Read labels.
> Rinse meats to decrease fat.
> Use reduced-fat and trans fat free butter.
> Replace salt with low-sodium seasonings.
> Take the stairs when possible.
> Substitute high-fat snacks with fruits and vegetables.
> Buy reduced-fat cheeses and low-fat milk and yogurt.
> Keep a food diary.
> Join an exercise club.

Unit 3   Clinical Nutrition and Therapeutic Diets

Chapter 17:   Nutrition for Clients with Diabetes Mellitus
Contributor: Lynne B. Welch, EdD, APRN, BC-FNP

⟲ NCLEX® Connections:

Learning Objective: Review and apply knowledge within "**Nutrition for Clients with Diabetes Mellitus**" in readiness for performance of the following nutrition nursing activities as outlined by the NCLEX® test plans:

Δ   Provide information to the client/family/significant other and/or reinforce client teaching on foods and prescribed dietary modifications appropriate in the management of diabetes.

Δ   Provide and/or help the client to maintain an appropriate diet based on a diagnosis of diabetes.

📖 Key Points

Δ   **Glucose** is the body's primary source of energy, and **insulin** is needed to assist the body in using glucose.

Δ   **Diabetes mellitus** inhibits the body's production and/or utilization of insulin. This results in above-normal glucose levels and **health complications** including heart disease, blindness, and renal (kidney) failure.

Δ   Achieving **proper nutrition** and meeting **specific dietary needs** is essential in controlling the effects of diabetes mellitus.

Δ   The goal of treatment is to assist the client in making the **appropriate lifestyle changes** and **nutritional choices** necessary to control blood glucose levels.

Δ   Blood glucose levels are used to diagnose diabetes.

Types of Diabetes

Δ   **Type 1 Diabetes Mellitus**

- Autoimmune, **genetically linked** disease.

- Characterized by inadequate production of insulin by the beta cells of the **pancreas**.

- Usually occurs in individuals under the age of 30 years.

△ **Type 2 Diabetes Mellitus**

- Result of **genetic** and **environmental factors**.

- Characterized by abnormal patterns of insulin secretion and decreased cellular uptake of glucose (**insulin resistance**).

- Usually occurs in individuals over the age of 40 years.

- **Obesity** and **sedentary lifestyle** are risk factors.

△ **Gestational Diabetes Mellitus (GDM)**

- **Glucose intolerance** that is recognized during **pregnancy**.

- Usually occurs during the **2nd** and **3rd trimesters**.

- Occurs only during pregnancy and typically resolves after delivery.

- Characterized by **increased insulin resistance** and **increased insulin antagonists**.

- Many women with GDM develop type 2 diabetes mellitus later in life.

- Blood glucose control is important for preventing damage to the fetus in women with pre-existing diabetes mellitus who are pregnant or those with GDM.

Alterations in Glucose Levels

△ **Hypoglycemia** is an **abnormally low** blood glucose level.

- It results from taking too much insulin, inadequate food intake, delayed or skipped meals, extra physical activity, or consumption of alcohol without food.

- Blood glucose levels of **70 mg/dL or less** require immediate action.

- **Symptoms** include mild shakiness, mental confusion, sweating, palpitations, headache, a lack of coordination, blurred vision, seizures, and coma.

- Individuals with hypoglycemia should be instructed to **take 15 g of readily absorbable carbohydrate**. Examples include:

  ◊ 2 or 3 glucose tablets.

  ◊ 5 Lifesavers™/hard candies.

  ◊ ½ cup (4 oz) juice or regular soda.

  ◊ 1 Tbsp of honey or brown sugar.

△ Retest the blood glucose in 15 min. If it is 50 to 80 mg/dL, then repeat the above steps. Once levels normalize, give an additional 15 g if the next meal is more than 1 hr away.

Δ **Hyperglycemia** is an **abnormally high** blood glucose level.

- It results from an imbalance among food, medication, and activity.

- **Symptoms** include blood glucose greater than 250 mg/dL, ketones in urine, polydipsia (excessive thirst), polyuria (excessive urination), hyperventilation, dehydration, fruity odor to breath, and coma.

- **Individuals with symptoms** of hyperglycemia should:

  ◊ Immediately consult their primary care provider, or go to the emergency department.

  ◊ Take their medicine if they have forgotten.

  ◊ Consider modifications to their insulin or oral diabetic medications.

- **Long-term implications** of untreated or inadequately treated hyperglycemia include blindness, kidney failure, dyslipidemia, hypertension, neuropathy, microvascular disease, and limb amputation.

Δ **Somagyi's phenomenon** is morning hyperglycemia in response to overnight hypoglycemia. Providing a bedtime snack and appropriate insulin dose will prevent hypoglycemia.

Δ **Dawn phenomenon** is an elevation of blood glucose around 0500 to 0600. It results from a overnight release of growth hormone, and it is treated by increasing the amount of insulin provided during the overnight hours.

Lifestyle and Diet Recommendations for Clients with Diabetes

Δ **Coronary heart disease (CHD)** is the leading cause of death among clients with diabetes. Therefore, clients with diabetes are encouraged to follow a diet that is high in fiber and low in saturated fat, trans fat, and cholesterol.

Δ **Dietary intake** should be **individualized**. General guidelines include:

- Encourage **complex carbohydrates** found in grains, fruits, and vegetables.

- Carbohydrates and monounsaturated fats combined should account for 60 to 70% of total calories.

- **Saturated fat** should account for **less than 10% of total calories**. If LDL is greater than 100 mg/dL, then saturated fat should be limited to less than 7% of intake.

- Promote **fiber** intake (beans, vegetables, oats, whole grains).

- **Protein** should comprise 15 to 20% of total caloric intake. Protein intake may need to be reduced in clients with diabetes and renal failure.

Δ Encourage clients with diabetes mellitus to **eliminate all tobacco use**.

Δ **Limit alcohol** intake and consume food with any alcohol consumption.

Δ **Encourage exercise**. Blood glucose levels and medication dosages should be closely monitored.

Δ Encourage **weight loss**.

- Weight loss is especially encouraged in clients with type 2 diabetes mellitus because it can decrease insulin resistance, improve glucose and lipid levels, and lower blood pressure.

Δ **Vitamin** and **mineral requirements** are unchanged for clients who have diabetes. Supplements are recommended for identified deficiencies. Deficiencies in magnesium and potassium can aggravate glucose intolerance.

Δ **Artificial sweeteners** are acceptable. Saccharin crosses the placenta and should be avoided during pregnancy.

Δ Clients should be encouraged to perform **self-monitoring** of their **blood glucose** levels.

- Strict control of glucose levels can reduce or postpone complications such as retinopathy, nephropathy, and neuropathy.

Δ Clients should be encouraged to receive **regular evaluations** from their primary care provider.

Δ Cultural and personal preferences should be considered in planning food intake.

Δ Client **education** and **support** should be provided for:

- Self-monitoring of blood glucose.
- Dietary and activity recommendations.
- Signs, symptoms, and treatment of hypoglycemia and hyperglycemia.
- Long-term complications of diabetes.
- Psychological implications.

Δ **Children with diabetes** will require parental support, guidance, and participation. Dietary intake must provide for proper growth and development.

Δ The American Diabetes Association and the American Dietetic Association developed a system of **exchange lists** for meal planning. These lists:

- Provide a framework that outlines dietary choices that are relatively consistent in total calories, carbohydrate, protein, and fat.
- Simplify the meal-planning process.
- Provide flexibility in food choices.
- Help to ensure consistent intake.
- Emphasize important nutritional concepts.

- Eliminate the need to calculate daily caloric intake.
- Do not eliminate the need for portion control.

Exchange List	Carbohydrate (grams)	Protein (grams)	Fat (grams)	cal	Example Foods
Starch	15	3	0-1	80	1 slice bread ½ cup corn ⅓ cup rice
Meat: Very Lean Lean Med Fat High Fat	0 0 0 0	7 7 7 7	0-1 3 5 8	35 55 75 100	1 oz poultry 1 oz sirloin 1 oz ground beef/1 egg 1 oz cheddar cheese
Vegetable	5	2	0	25	½ cup cooked, 1 cup raw
Fruit	15	0	0	60	1 small apple 17 grapes ½ cup juice
Milk: Skim 2 percent Whole	12 12 12	8 8 8	0-3 5 8	90 120 150	1 cup non-fat yogurt 1 cup low-fat yogurt
Fat (all)	0	0	5	45	1 tsp oil, butter/ 1 slice bacon

Primary Reference:

Dudek, S. G. (2006). *Nutrition essentials for nursing practice* (5th ed.). Philadelphia: Lippincott Williams & Wilkins.

Additional Resources:

Grosvenor, M.B., & Smolin, L.A. (2002). *Nutrition: From science to life.* Indianapolis, IN: Wiley.

Mahan, L. K., & Escott-Stump, S. (1996). *Krause's food, nutrition and diet therapy* (10th ed.). Philadelphia: W.B. Saunders Company.

Stanfield, P. S., & Hui, Y. H. (2003). *Nutrition and diet therapy: Self-instructional modules* (4th ed.). Sudbury, MA: Jones and Bartlett Publishers.

For more information, visit the American Diabetes Association at: *www.diabetes.org.*

Chapter 17: Nutrition for Clients with Diabetes Mellitus

Application Exercises

1. A nurse is caring for a 7-year-old boy who is newly diagnosed with type 1 diabetes mellitus. His mother states that she is concerned about the implications of the diabetes, which she does not fully understand. What information is important to share with this client?

2. Which of the following symptoms suggest hypoglycemia in a client with diabetes mellitus? (Check all that apply.)

_____ Fruity odor to breath

_____ Blurred vision

_____ Seizures

_____ Headache

_____ Vomiting

_____ Diarrhea

_____ Fever

_____ Hyper-excitability

_____ Shakiness

_____ Sweating

_____ Mental confusion

3. **True or False:** If a woman develops GDM during pregnancy, she will continue to be diabetic following delivery.

4. **True or False:** Type 2 diabetes mellitus is a genetically linked disease that leads to inadequate production of insulin by the beta cells of the pancreas.

5. **True or False:** Renal failure is the leading cause of death in clients with diabetes mellitus.

6. **True or False:** A release of growth hormone contributes to the hyperglycemia that occurs with dawn phenomenon.

7. A nurse is caring for a 53-year-old client with diabetes mellitus. The client reports being dizzy, lightheaded, and seeing "two of everything." What is this client likely experiencing? What interventions should the nurse perform?

Chapter 17: Nutrition for Clients with Diabetes Mellitus

Application Exercises Answer Key

1. A nurse is caring for a 7-year-old boy who is newly diagnosed with type 1 diabetes mellitus. His mother states that she is concerned about the implications of the diabetes, which she does not fully understand. What information is important to share with this client?

   The nurse should first acknowledge the mother's concerns, reassure her that they are normal, and provide support. The mother should be informed that close monitoring and strict control of blood glucose levels in clients with diabetes mellitus can delay the onset and development of any long-term complications. Share the appropriate dietary guidelines for fat, protein, and carbohydrate consumption. Educate her regarding the signs, symptoms, and treatment of hypoglycemia and hyperglycemia. Lastly, the nurse should provide the mother with educational materials and resources, such as the American Diabetes Association, the American Dietetic Association, or a local support group for parents of children with diabetes mellitus.

2. Which of the following symptoms suggest hypoglycemia in a client with diabetes mellitus? (Check all that apply.)

   _____ Fruity odor to breath

   __x__ Blurred vision

   __x__ Seizures

   __x__ Headache

   _____ Vomiting

   _____ Diarrhea

   _____ Fever

   _____ Hyper-excitability

   __x__ Shakiness

   __x__ Sweating

   __x__ Mental confusion

3. **True or False:** If a woman develops GDM during pregnancy, she will continue to be diabetic following delivery.

   False: While many women with GDM develop type 2 diabetes mellitus later in life, this is not true for all women.

4. **True or False:** Type 2 diabetes mellitus is a genetically linked disease that leads to inadequate production of insulin by the beta cells of the pancreas.

False: These are characteristics of type 1 diabetes mellitus. Type 2 diabetes mellitus is characterized by abnormal patterns of insulin secretion and insulin resistance and is caused by combination of genetic and environmental factors.

5. **True or False:** Renal failure is the leading cause of death in clients with diabetes mellitus.

False: CHD is the leading cause of death in people with diabetes mellitus.

6. **True or False:** A release of growth hormone contributes to the hyperglycemia that occurs with dawn phenomenon.

True

7. A nurse is caring for a 53-year-old client with diabetes mellitus. The client reports being dizzy, lightheaded, and seeing "two of everything." What is this client likely experiencing? What interventions should the nurse perform?

This client is experiencing symptoms of hypoglycemia. The nurse should first perform a blood glucose test. Once hypoglycemia is confirmed as the cause, the nurse should instruct the client to take 15 g of readily absorbable glucose (2 or 3 glucose tablets, 5 hard candies, ½ cup or 4 oz of juice, or 1 Tbsp of honey or brown sugar). Recheck the client's blood glucose in 15 min. If it is above 80 mg/dL, follow with an additional 15 g if meal time is more than 1 hr away.

Unit 3   Clinical Nutrition and Therapeutic Diets

Chapter 18:   Nutrition for Clients with Renal Disorders
                    Contributor: Dana Bartlett, MSN, RN, CSPI

NCLEX® Connections:

Learning Objective: Review and apply knowledge within "**Nutrition for Clients with Renal Disorders**" in readiness for performance of the following nutrition nursing activities as outlined by the NCLEX® test plans:

Δ   Provide information to the client/family/significant other and/or reinforce client teaching on foods and prescribed dietary modifications appropriate in the management of renal disorders.

Δ   Provide and/or help the client to maintain an appropriate diet based on a diagnosis of a renal disease.

Key Points

Δ   The **kidneys** have two basic functions: they **maintain normal blood volume and excrete waste products**.

Δ   Loss of renal function and/or renal damage can cause profound effects on the nutritional state.

Δ   **Urea** is a waste byproduct of protein metabolism. Urea levels rise with renal disease. Therefore, **monitoring protein intake** is paramount for these clients.

Δ   **Short-term renal disease** requires nutritional support for healing rather than dietary restrictions.

Δ   Dietary recommendations are dependent upon the stage of renal disease.

Renal Diseases and Nutritional Guidelines

Δ   **Pre-End Stage Renal Disease (pre-ESRD)**

•   Pre-ESRD, or diminished renal reserve/renal insufficiency, is a **predialysis condition** distinguished by an **increase in serum creatinine**.

- Goals of **nutritional therapy** for pre-ESRD are to:

  ◊ Control blood glucose levels and hypertension, which are both risk factors.

  ◊ Help preserve remaining renal function by **limiting** the intake of **protein** and **phosphorus**.

- **Restricting phosphorus** intake slows the progression of renal disease.

  ◊ High levels of phosphorus contribute to calcium and phosphorus deposits in the kidneys.

- **Protein restriction** is key for clients with pre-ESRD.

  ◊ Slows the progression of renal disease.

  ◊ Too little protein results in breakdown of body protein, so protein intake must be carefully determined.

- **Dietary recommendations** for pre-ESRD:

  ◊ Restrict sodium intake to maintain blood pressure.

  ◊ Limit meat intake.

  ◊ Limit dairy products to ½ cup per day.

  ◊ Limit high-phosphorus foods (peanut butter, dried peas and beans, bran, cola, chocolate, beer, some whole grains).

  ◊ Caution clients to use vitamin and mineral supplements ONLY when recommended by their provider.

Δ **End Stage Renal Disease (ESRD)**

- ESRD, or chronic renal failure, occurs when the **glomerular filtration rate (GFR)** is less than 25 mL/min, the **serum creatinine level** steadily rises, or **dialysis or transplantation** is necessary.

- The goal of nutritional therapy is to **maintain appropriate fluid status**, **blood pressure**, and **blood chemistries**.

  ◊ A high-protein, low-phosphorus, low-potassium, low-sodium, fluid-restricted diet is recommended.

  ◊ Calcium and vitamin D are nutrients of concern.

- **Potassium intake** is dependent upon the client's laboratory values, which should be closely monitored.

- **Sodium and fluid** allowances are determined by blood pressure, weight, serum electrolyte levels, and urine output.

- Achieving a well-balanced diet based on the above guidelines is a difficult task. The National Renal Diet provides clients with a list of appropriate food choices.

- **Protein needs increase** once dialysis is begun because protein and amino acids are lost in the dialysate.

  ◊ Fifty percent of protein intake should come from biologic sources (milk, meat, fish, poultry, soy, eggs).

  ◊ Adequate calories (35 cal/kg of body weight) should be consumed to maintain body protein stores.

- **Phosphorus** must be **restricted**.

  ◊ The high protein requirement leads to an increase in phosphorus intake.

  ◊ Phosphate binders must be taken with all meals and snacks.

- **Vitamin D deficiency** occurs because the kidneys are unable to convert it to its active form.

  ◊ This alters the metabolism of calcium, phosphorus, and magnesium and leads to hyperphosphatemia, hypocalcemia, and hypermagnesemia.

  ◊ Calcium supplements will likely be required because foods high in phosphorus (which are restricted) are also high in calcium.

Δ **Acute Renal Failure (ARF)**

- ARF is an **abrupt, rapid decline** in renal function. It is usually caused by trauma, sepsis, poor perfusion, or medications. ARF can cause hyponatremia, hyperkalemia, hypocalcemia, and hyperphosphatemia.

- Diet therapy for ARF is dependent upon the phase of ARF and its underlying cause.

Δ **Nephrotic Syndrome**

- Nephrotic syndrome results in **serum proteins leaking into the urine**.

- Nutritional therapy goals include minimizing edema, replacing lost nutrients, and minimizing renal damage. Dietary recommendations indicate sufficient protein and low-sodium intake.

Δ **Nephrolithiasis (Kidney Stones)**

- **Increasing fluid consumption** is the primary intervention for the treatment and prevention of the formation of renal calculi.

- Excessive intake of protein, sodium, calcium, and oxalates (rhubarb, spinach, beets) may increase the risk of stone formation.

Additional Nursing Assessments/Data Collection for Clients with Renal Disease

Δ   The nurse should monitor the **client's weight daily** or more frequently as prescribed. This is an **indicator of fluid status,** a primary concern for these clients.

Δ   Monitor the client's **fluid intake** and encourage compliance with fluid restrictions.

Δ   The nurse should monitor **urine output**. Placement of a **Foley catheter** may be necessary for accurate measurement.

Δ   Monitor for signs and symptoms of **constipation**. Fluid restrictions predispose clients to constipation.

Δ   Explain to the client why dietary changes are necessary.

Δ   Provide support for the client and family.

Primary Reference:

Dudek, S. G. (2006). *Nutrition essentials for nursing practice* (5th ed.). Philadelphia: Lippincott Williams & Wilkins.

Additional Resources:

Beers, M. H., & Berkow, R. (Eds.): (1999). *The Merck manual of diagnosis and therapy* (17th ed.). Indianapolis, IN: Wiley.

For more information, visit the National Kidney Foundation at: *www.kidney.org.*

Chapter 18: Nutrition for Clients with Renal Disorders

Application Exercises

1. A nurse is caring for a client who is newly diagnosed with pre-ESRD. The client states that he is hungry. Which of the following foods would be an appropriate choice for this client? (Check all that apply.)

     _____ Peanut butter sandwich with skim milk

     _____ Single slice of cheese with reduced-sodium crackers

     _____ Can of cola

     _____ Dish of cantaloupe

     _____ White toast with jelly

2. A client with pre-ESRD is preparing for discharge from the hospital. His wife arrives to escort him home. What general guidelines should the nurse share with the client and his spouse?

3. **True or False:** Protein should be restricted in clients with ESRD.

4. **True or False:** Food sources of calcium are preferred over calcium supplements for clients with ESRD.

5. **True or False:** Low sodium and sufficient protein intake are recommended for clients with nephrotic syndrome.

6. A nurse is completing the initial assessment of a client. Her past medical history indicates that this client has a history of ESRD and undergoes dialysis three times per week. What initial and ongoing assessment data should the nurse collect?

Chapter 18: Nutrition for Clients with Renal Disorders

Application Exercises Answer Key

1. A nurse is caring for a client who is newly diagnosed with pre-ESRD. The client states that he is hungry. Which of the following foods would be an appropriate choice for this client? (Check all that apply.)

           Peanut butter sandwich with skim milk

   x   Single slice of cheese with reduced-sodium crackers

           Can of cola

   x   Dish of cantaloupe

   x   White toast with jelly

2. A client with pre-ESRD is preparing for discharge from the hospital. His wife arrives to escort him home. What general guidelines should the nurse share with the client and his spouse?

The nurse should explain to the client and his spouse why the dietary recommendations are necessary. The nurse should instruct the client that consuming a diet low in protein and phosphorus can slow the progression of renal disease. The nurse should educate the client about foods that are high in protein and phosphorus (dairy products, meats, peanut butter, beans). The nurse should caution the client to use vitamin and mineral supplements only when recommended by the provider.

3. **True or False:** Protein should be restricted in clients with ESRD.

False: Protein needs are increased in ESRD because proteins and amino acids are lost in the dialysate. Protein and phosphorus intake are decreased in pre-ESRD.

4. **True or False:** Food sources of calcium are preferred over calcium supplements for clients with ESRD.

False: Foods high in calcium, namely dairy products, are also high in phosphorus, which should be restricted for client with ESRD. Therefore, calcium supplements are preferred to achieve adequate calcium intake.

5. **True or False:** Low sodium and sufficient protein intake are recommended for clients with nephrotic syndrome.

   True

6. A nurse is completing the initial assessment of a client. Her past medical history indicates that this client has a history of ESRD and undergoes dialysis three times per week. What initial and ongoing assessment data should the nurse collect?

   The nurse should monitor the following:

   Δ   Daily weights.

   Δ   Intake and output.

   Δ   Signs of constipation.

   Δ   BUN, creatinine, and electrolytes.

   All of the above are important indicators of clients with any renal disease.

Unit 3   Clinical Nutrition and Therapeutic Diets

Chapter 19:   Nutrition for Clients with Cancer or HIV/AIDS
                Contributor: Jackie H. Jones, EdD, RN

⟳ NCLEX® Connections:

> **Learning Objective**: Review and apply knowledge within "**Nutrition for Clients with Cancer or HIV/AIDS**" in readiness for performance of the following nutrition nursing activities as outlined by the NCLEX® test plans:
>
> Δ   Provide information to the client/family/significant other and/or reinforce client teaching on foods and prescribed dietary modifications appropriate in the management of cancer.
>
> Δ   Provide and/or help the client to maintain an appropriate diet based on a diagnosis of cancer.
>
> Δ   Provide information to the client/family/significant other and/or reinforce client teaching on foods and prescribed dietary modifications appropriate in the management of HIV/AIDS.
>
> Δ   Provide and/or help the client to maintain an appropriate diet based on a diagnosis of HIV/AIDS.

▱ Key Points

Δ   Environmental agents, genetic factors, and immune system function relate to the **development of cancer**.

Δ   Major **treatments for cancer** include surgery, radiation, chemotherapy, immunotherapy, and bone marrow transplantation. Side effects of these treatments **compromise the nutritional status of affected clients**.

Δ   Autoimmune deficiency syndrome (**AIDS**) is a life-threatening disease caused by human immunodeficiency virus (**HIV**), a retrovirus that attacks T-cells and causes a **severe depression of immune function**.

Δ   **Protein-calorie malnutrition** and **body wasting** are common problems for clients with cancer and HIV/AIDS and are a major cause of morbidity and mortality.

Δ   The goals of **nutritional therapy** are to: minimize the nutritional complications of disease, improve nutritional status, prevent muscle wasting, maintain weight, promote healing, reduce side effects, decrease morbidity and mortality, and enhance quality of life and the overall effectiveness of treatment therapies.

Δ   Nutritional plans are individualized for client needs.

Δ   More than one-third of all cancer deaths are related to nutritional complications.

Δ   Diet is a key factor in the treatment and prevention of cancer.

Nutritional Guidelines to Aid Cancer Prevention

Δ   Adequate **dietary fiber** may lessen the risk of colon cancer.

Δ   Eliminate all tobacco to reduce the risk of lung cancer.

Δ   **High intake of fruits and vegetables** is linked to a lowered incidence of many types of cancer. Eat at least 5 servings daily.

Δ   Consume **whole grains** rather than processed or refined grains or sugars.

Δ   Meat preparation by smoking, pickling, charcoal grilling, and use of nitrate-containing chemicals may be carcinogenic.

Δ   High intake of **polyunsaturated** and **monounsaturated fats** in fish and olive oils is presumed to be beneficial in **lowering the risk** of many types of cancer.

Δ   High alcohol consumption is associated with liver, pancreatic, and biliary cancers.

Δ   **Excess body fat** stimulates the production of estrogen and progesterone, which may intensify the growth of various cell types and may contribute to breast, gallbladder, colon, prostate, uterine, and kidney cancers.

Δ   A **calcium-rich diet** is associated with a lower incidence of colon cancer because it binds free fatty acids and bile salts in the lower gastrointestinal tract.

Nutritional Considerations for Clients with Cancer

Δ   Cancer may cause **anorexia, increased metabolism, and negative nitrogen balance**.

Δ   Systemic effects result in **poor food intake, increased nutrient and energy needs, and catabolism of body tissues**.

Δ   Nutritional plans are individualized according to client needs.

Δ **Nutritional needs** for the client with cancer include:

- Increased caloric intake ranging from 25 to 35 cal/kg to maintain weight and 40 to 50 cal/kg to rebuild body stores.

- Protein needs are increased to 1.5 to 2.0 g/kg.

- Vitamin and mineral supplementation is based upon client need.

Δ **Complications** associated with nutritional management include:

- Early satiety.

- Mouth ulcers and stomatitis.

- Fatigue.

- Food aversions.

- Taste alterations and thick saliva.

- Gastrointestinal problems such as nausea, vomiting, and diarrhea.

Strategies to Promote the Nutritional Status of Clients with Cancer

Δ Encourage clients to eat more on "good" days.

Δ Encourage intake of foods that have been modified to contain **additional protein and calories**. Foods choices include:

- Milk, cheese, milkshakes, and pudding.

- Fish.

- Eggs.

- Nuts.

Δ **Supplements** that are high in protein and/or calories should be encouraged.

- These supplements should be offered between meals and can be used as meal replacements if necessary.

Δ **Increase protein and caloric content** of foods by:

- Substituting whole milk for water in recipes.

- Adding cheese to dishes.

- Using peanut butter as a spread for fruits.

- Using yogurt as a topping for fruit.

- Dipping meats in milk and bread crumbs before cooking.

Δ A **high-carbohydrate diet** provides needed energy without an extended feeling of satiety.

Δ   **High-fat foods** provide a feeling of fullness and remain in the stomach longer than carbohydrate foods.

Δ   To help **control nausea**, encourage the client to eat high-carbohydrate, low-fat foods such as:

- Yogurt.

- Cooked cereals.

- Toast or crackers.

- Sherbet.

- Canned fruits.

- Fruit juices.

- Bananas.

Δ   For clients with **diarrhea**, the nurse should:

- Encourage foods high in pectin and other soluble fibers (oatmeal, bananas, applesauce) as they may slow transit time through the colon.

- Replace fluid and electrolytes with clear liquids such as:
  - ◊ Sports drinks.
  - ◊ Soups.
  - ◊ Broth.

- Avoid gaseous-producing foods and liquids such as beans, carbonated beverages, and cruciferous vegetables (broccoli, cabbage, brussels sprouts).

- Promote fluid intake.

Δ   Chronic **dehydration** contributes to fatigue.

Δ   Fluids stimulate salivary secretions and the moisture necessary for digestion.

Δ   Limit liquids with meals to avoid early satiety and bloating at mealtime.

Δ   A client receiving immunosuppressant therapy may need to **minimize exposure to microorganisms** found on the outer layers of fresh fruits and vegetables. Peeling and thorough washing or cooking may be necessary. In some cases, fresh foods may increase the risk of infection.

Δ   For clients experiencing **stomatitis (mouth sores)**, the nurse should:

- Provide foods that are soft and relatively bland.

- Avoid hot foods and beverages.

- Provide cold items that may help numb the oral mucosa.

- Encourage the use of straws and meticulous oral care.

△ To reduce **metallic taste** in foods, encourage the caregiver to prepare foods using plastic utensils.

△ Serve foods in an attractive manner to increase the appeal. **Small, frequent servings** are advised.

△ To combat **dysphagia**, the nurse may teach the client to inhale, swallow, and then exhale. Also, tilting of the head may help with swallowing. Avoiding sticky or lumpy food is advised.

△ Clients experiencing **thick saliva** should be encouraged to avoid foods that are dry, coarse, or sticky. Utilizing ice chips or hard candies may alleviate dryness between meals.

Nutritional Considerations for Clients with HIV/AIDS

△ The **body's response** to the inflammatory and immune processes associated with HIV **increases nutrient requirements**; therefore, malnutrition is a common problem and is one of the causes of death in AIDS.

△ HIV infection, secondary infection, malignancies, and medication therapies can cause symptoms and side effects that **impair intake and alter metabolism**.

△ Overall, **caloric needs are increased**, generally ranging from 35 to 45 cal/kg.

△ A **high-protein** diet is recommended with amounts varying from 1.2 to 2.0 g/kg.

△ One or two multivitamin and mineral tablets a day are recommended unless a specific deficiency is identified.

△ Poor nutritional status leads to wasting and fever, further aggravating the susceptibility to secondary infections.

△ **Wasting** is distinguished by an unintended **weight loss of 10%** and concurrent problems that include diarrhea or chronic weakness and fever for at least 30 days.

△ Decreased nutrient intake occurs because of **physical symptoms** such as anorexia, nausea, vomiting, and diarrhea. **Psychological symptoms** may include depression and dementia.

△ **Diarrhea and malabsorption** are prominent clinical problems in persons with AIDS.

△ Liberal fluid intake is extremely important to prevent dehydration.

△ **Nutritional warning signs** in clients with HIV/AIDS include rapid weight loss, gastrointestinal problems, inadequate intake, increased nutrient needs, food aversions, fad diets, and supplements.

△ If the client with AIDS is unable to consume sufficient nutrients, calories, and fluid, **enteral feedings** may be needed.

Strategies to Promote the Nutritional Status of Clients with HIV/AIDS

Δ   Encourage the client to consume **small, frequent meals** that are composed of **high-protein, high-calorie,** and **nutrient-dense foods** (see high-protein and high-calorie foods listed under "Strategies to Promote the Nutritional Status of Clients with Cancer.")

Δ   Utilize interventions described under "Strategies to Promote the Nutritional Status of Clients with Cancer" for those clients suffering from nausea, vomiting, diarrhea, and anorexia.

Additional Interventions

Δ   For clients with cancer and/or HIV/AIDS, the nurse should:

- Obtain **baseline assessment data**, such as weight, body mass index, height, nutritional habits, recent weight trends, disease history, food preferences, and pertinent laboratory values (albumin, ferritin).

- Continue to monitor these assessment parameters during the course of treatment.

- Provide education for the client regarding **expected symptoms and side effects** of treatments and their effects on **nutritional requirements** and patterns.

- Educate the client and his or her support system regarding **nutritional recommendations** and the appropriate food choices.

- Assist the client with establishing realistic nutritional goals and discuss ways to increase consumption.

- Provide support to the client and his or her support system.

Primary Reference:

Dudek, S. G. (2006). *Nutrition essentials for nursing practice* (5th ed.). Philadelphia: Lippincott Williams & Wilkins.

Additional Resources:

Roth, R. A., & Townsend, C. E. (2003). *Nutrition & diet therapy* (8th ed.). Clifton Park, NY: Thomson Delmar Learning.

Stanfield, P. S., & Hui, Y. H. (2003). *Nutrition and diet therapy: Self-instructional modules* (4th ed.). Sudbury, MA: Jones and Bartlett Publishers.

For more information about cancer, visit the American Cancer Society at: *www.cancer.org* or the National Cancer Institute at: *www.cancer.gov*.

For more information about HIV/AIDS, visit AIDS.org at: *www.aids.org*, the Association of Nutrition Services Agencies at: *www.aidsnutrition.org*, or the Office of AIDS Research at: *www.nih.gov/od/oar/*.

Chapter 19: Nutrition for Clients with Cancer or HIV/AIDS

Application Exercises

Scenario: A nurse is caring for a 28-year-old female client who has recently been diagnosed with Hodgkin's lymphoma. She undergoes chemotherapy every 2 weeks, and she has had two treatments thus far.

1. The client reports that she rarely eats more than two meals per day. She states that she is too tired and that nothing sounds good. What information regarding nutritional requirements is important to share with her?

2. After educating her as to appropriate food choices based on her body's needs, the nurse determines that the client understands the information when she chooses which of the following snacks? (Check all that apply.)

   _____ Peanut butter sandwich on whole wheat bread with 2% milk

   _____ Popcorn with soda

   _____ Yogurt topped with granola and banana

   _____ Meat lasagna with buttered garlic bread

   _____ Plain baked potato

   _____ Donut with coffee

   _____ Cottage cheese with canned peaches

3. **True or False:** Meats that are pickled, smoked, or grilled over charcoal may be carcinogenic.

4. **True or False:** Saturated fat is the preferred fat to consume to aid in the prevention of cancer.

5. **True or False:** Cold foods may provide comfort for clients suffering from stomatitis.

6. **True or False:** Clients with cancer or HIV/AIDS should be encouraged to consume large amounts of fluid.

Scenario: A nurse is caring for a 41-year-old male client who has AIDS. During the assessment, he reveal that he has suffered from nausea, vomiting, and diarrhea for the last 3 weeks. He states that he feels very weak and no longer has the energy to finish any task.

7. What guidance should the nurse provide to him regarding appropriate food choices to combat his symptoms?

8. If his symptoms do not improve, what should the nurse expect as the next step for this client?

Chapter 19: Nutrition for Clients with Cancer or HIV/AIDS

Application Exercises Answer Key

Scenario: A nurse is caring for a 28-year-old female client who has recently been diagnosed with Hodgkin's lymphoma. She undergoes chemotherapy every 2 weeks, and she has had two treatments thus far.

1. The client reports that she rarely eats more than two meals per day. She states that she is too tired and that nothing sounds good. What information regarding nutritional requirements is important to share with her?

   The nurse should first acknowledge the client's feelings and provide her with an opportunity to share her frustrations. It is important to instruct her that her cancer and her chemotherapy are placing demands on her body that require an increase in protein and caloric intake. Encourage her to eat more when she is feeling better (on "good" days). Assist her in developing some realistically achievable nutritional intake goals. Instruct her on food sources that are high in protein and high in calories. Also, provide the client with methods for increasing her caloric intake with her regular food choices (add cheese to meals, use higher fat milk, use peanut butter as a spread).

2. After educating her as to appropriate food choices based on her body's needs, the nurse determines that the client understands the information when she chooses which of the following snacks? (Check all that apply.)

   __x__ Peanut butter sandwich on whole wheat bread with 2% milk

   _____ Popcorn with soda

   __x__ Yogurt topped with granola and banana

   __x__ Meat lasagna with buttered garlic bread

   _____ Plain baked potato

   _____ Donut with coffee

   __x__ Cottage cheese with canned peaches

3. **True or False:** Meats that are pickled, smoked, or grilled over charcoal may be carcinogenic.

   True

4. **True or False:** Saturated fat is the preferred fat to consume to aid in the prevention of cancer.

False: Monounsaturated and polyunsaturated fats are presumed to be beneficial in lowering the risk of many types of cancer. They are found in fish and olive oil.

5. **True or False:** Cold foods may provide comfort for clients suffering from stomatitis.

True

6. **True or False:** Clients with cancer or HIV/AIDS should be encouraged to consume large amounts of fluid.

True

Scenario: A nurse is caring for a 41-year-old male client who has AIDS. During the assessment, he reveals that he has suffered from nausea, vomiting, and diarrhea for the last 3 weeks. He states that he feels very weak and no longer has the energy to finish any task.

---

7. What guidance should the nurse provide to him regarding appropriate food choices to combat his symptoms?

The nurse should encourage the client to eat high-carbohydrate, low-fat foods as they may help with nausea. Examples include toast or crackers, yogurt, bananas, canned fruits, and cooked cereals. The client should also be instructed on the importance of replacing fluids. Broths, soups, sports drinks, and canned fruits provide the client with calories and valuable electrolytes. Nutritional supplements may be recommended if the client is able to tolerate them.

8. If his symptoms do not improve, what should the nurse expect as the next step for this client?

When clients with HIV/AIDS are unable to consume enough calories, enteral feedings may be indicated. This is also true of clients with cancer.

Unit 3   Clinical Nutrition and Therapeutic Diets

Chapter 20:   Nutrition for Clients with Anemia

Contributor: Pamela Y. Mahon, PhD, RN

⟳ NCLEX® Connections:

Learning Objective: Review and apply knowledge within "**Nutrition for Clients with Anemia**" in readiness for performance of the following nutrition nursing activities as outlined by the NCLEX® test plans:

Δ   Provide information to the client/family/significant other and/or reinforce client teaching on foods and prescribed dietary modifications appropriate in the prevention and/or management of anemia.

Δ   Provide and/or help the client to maintain an appropriate diet based on a diagnosis of anemia.

📖 Key Points

Δ   Anemia results from either a **reduction** in the number of **red blood cells (RBCs)** or in **hemoglobin,** the oxygen-carrying component of blood.

Δ   Anemia can result from a decrease in RBC production, an increase in RBC destruction, or a loss of blood.

Δ   The body requires **iron**, **vitamin B$_{12}$**, and **folic acid** to produce red blood cells.

Δ   **Iron deficiency anemia** is the most common nutritional disorder in the world. It affects approximately **10% of the U.S. population**, especially older infants, toddlers, adolescent girls, and pregnant women.

Δ   From childhood until adolescence, iron intake tends to be marginal.

Δ   **Pernicious anemia** is the most common form of **vitamin B$_{12}$ deficiency**. It is caused by lack of **intrinsic factor**, a protein that helps the body absorb vitamin B$_{12}$. Risk factors include gastric surgery, gastric cancer, *Helicobacter pylori*, and age greater than 50. Clients with pernicious anemia require vitamin B$_{12}$ injections.

Classifications of Anemia and Nursing Assessments/Data Collection and Interventions

Δ **Iron deficiency anemia** can result from poor intestinal absorption, blood loss, and inadequate consumption.

- **Symptoms**
  - ◊ Fatigue
  - ◊ Lethargy
  - ◊ Pallor of nail beds
  - ◊ Intolerance to cold

- **Sources of Iron**
  - ◊ Beef liver
  - ◊ Red meat
  - ◊ Fish
  - ◊ Poultry
  - ◊ Tofu
  - ◊ Dried peas and beans
  - ◊ Whole grains
  - ◊ Dried fruit

- **Iron-Fortified Foods**
  - ◊ Infant formula (acceptable alternative or supplement to breastfeeding)
  - ◊ Infant cereal (usually the first food introduced to infants)
  - ◊ Ready-to-eat cereals

- **Vitamin C** facilitates the absorption of iron (promote consumption).

- **Children** with low iron intake can present with short attention spans and show poor intellectual performance even before the anemia begins.

- **Caution**: *Medicinal iron overdose is the leading cause of accidental poisoning in small children and can lead to acute iron toxicity.*

Δ **Vitamin B$_{12}$ deficiency anemia** results from a failure to absorb vitamin B$_{12}$ (pernicious anemia) or inadequate intake. Manifestations include fatigue as well as gastrointestinal and neurological symptoms.

- **Gastrointestinal Symptoms**
  - ◊ Glossitis (inflamed tongue)
  - ◊ Anorexia
  - ◊ Indigestion
  - ◊ Weight loss

- **Neurological Symptoms**
  - ◊ Paresthesia (numbness) of hands/feet
  - ◊ Decreased proprioception (sense of body position)
  - ◊ Poor muscle coordination
  - ◊ Increasing irritability
  - ◊ Delirium

- **Natural Sources of Vitamin B$_{12}$**
  - ◊ Fish
  - ◊ Meat
  - ◊ Poultry
  - ◊ Eggs
  - ◊ Milk

- People over the age of 50 are urged to consume most of their vitamin B$_{12}$ requirement from supplements or fortified food.

- **Vegans** need supplemental B$_{12}$.

Δ **Folic acid deficiency anemia** is caused by poor nutrition, malabsorption (Crohn's disease), and drug use. Manifestations include mental confusion, fainting, fatigue, and gastrointestinal distress.

- **Symptoms** of folic acid deficiency anemia mimic those for vitamin B$_{12}$ deficiency anemia *except* for the *neurological symptoms*.

- **Folic Acid Sources**
  - ◊ Green leafy vegetables
  - ◊ Dried peas and beans
  - ◊ Liver
  - ◊ Seeds
  - ◊ Orange juice
  - ◊ Cereals and breads fortified with folic acid are also good choices.

- If the client is unable to obtain an adequate supply of folic acid, **supplementation** may be necessary.

Primary Reference:

Dudek, S. G. (2006). *Nutrition essentials for nursing practice* (5th ed.). Philadelphia: Lippincott Williams & Wilkins.

Additional Resources:

Potter, P. A., & Perry, A. G. (2005). *Fundamentals of nursing* (6th ed.). St. Louis, MO: Mosby.

Chapter 20: Nutrition for Clients with Anemia

Application Exercises

Scenario: A nurse is caring for a 13-year-old female client. She states that she has been feeling tired and is having trouble maintaining her attention span in school. Further assessment yields that she began menstruating 6 months ago.

1. These symptoms are indicative of what condition?

2. The nurse should provide what education regarding iron intake?

3. **True or False:** Vegans require folic acid supplementation.

4. **True or False:** Vitamin B_{12} is necessary for normal neurological functioning.

5. **True or False:** Nail bed pallor and intolerance to cold are signs of iron deficiency anemia.

Scenario: A 57-year-old male client is being seen for his annual physical. He states that he has felt fatigued over the last 6 weeks and that he has been experiencing numbness in his hands.

6. These symptoms are indicative of what condition?

7. The nurse assists the client in determining his typical daily food intake. He eats eggs each morning for breakfast and drinks milk with every meal. The client additionally states that he eats red meat at least every other day. Given the client's diet history, what is the likely cause of his anemia? What is the expected course of treatment?

8. Which of the following foods are good sources of vitamin B_{12}? (Check all that apply.)

_____ Beef liver

_____ Broccoli

_____ Salmon

_____ Apples

_____ Eggs

_____ Yogurt

Chapter 20: Nutrition for Clients with Anemia

Application Exercises Answer Key

Scenario: A nurse is caring for a 13-year-old female client. She states that she has been feeling tired and is having trouble maintaining her attention span in school. Further assessment yields that she began menstruating 6 months ago.

1. These symptoms are indicative of what condition?

   This client's symptoms are indicative of iron deficiency anemia. Fatigue and nail bed pallor are two signs of iron deficiency anemia. Additionally, iron deficiency anemia is prevalent among adolescent girls, and it can result from blood loss experienced during menstruation.

2. The nurse should provide what education regarding iron intake?

   The nurse should first explain that iron deficiency is common among adolescent females, and then instruct the client on recognizing the signs and symptoms of the disorder. The nurse should encourage the client to incorporate iron-rich foods (meats, fish, beans, whole grains, dried fruit) into her diet to achieve adequate iron intake.

3. **True or False:** Vegans require folic acid supplementation.

   False: Vegans require vitamin B_{12} supplementation because their diet lacks the food sources that contain the vitamin, such as fish, meat, eggs, and milk. Vegan diets are often rich in folic acid because the diet often contains large amounts of green leafy vegetables, beans, peas, and seeds. All of these foods are rich in folic acid.

4. **True or False:** Vitamin B_{12} is necessary for normal neurological functioning.

   True

5. **True or False:** Nail bed pallor and intolerance to cold are signs of iron deficiency anemia.

True

Scenario: A 57-year-old male client is being seen for his annual physical. He states that he has felt fatigued over the last 6 weeks and that he has been experiencing numbness in his hands.

6. These symptoms are indicative of what condition?

Vitamin B$_{12}$ deficiency anemia

7. The nurse assists the client in determining his typical daily food intake. He eats eggs each morning for breakfast and drinks milk with every meal. The client additionally states that he eats red meat at least every other day. Given the client's diet history, what is the likely cause of his anemia? What is the expected course of treatment?

The client's anemia is likely the result of an inability to absorb vitamin B$_{12}$ due to a lack of intrinsic factor, which is known as pernicious anemia. The client will need vitamin B$_{12}$ injections.

8. Which of the following foods are good sources of vitamin B$_{12}$? (Check all that apply.)

    __x__ Beef liver

    _____ Broccoli

    __x__ Salmon

    _____ Apples

    __x__ Eggs

    __x__ Yogurt